THE
DEATH
OF
LIBERALISM

THE
DEATH
OF
LIBERALISM

R. EMMETT TYRRELL, JR.

THOMAS NELSON
Since 1798

NASHVILLE   DALLAS   MEXICO CITY   RIO DE JANEIRO

Published in Nashville, Tennessee, by Thomas Nelson. Thomas Nelson is a registered trademark of Thomas Nelson, Inc.

Thomas Nelson, Inc., titles may be purchased in bulk for educational, business, fundraising, or sales promotional use. For information, please e-mail SpecialMarkets@ ThomasNelson.com.

Library of Congress Control Number: 2012933210

978-1-59555-488-8

Printed in the United States of America

12 13 14 15 QGF 6 5 4 3 2 1

For Larry Auriana,
Stalwart of the Board of Directors,

and

Wlady Pleszczynski,
who knows where all the bodies are buried.

CONTENTS

INTRODUCTION

I n the introduction to my 2010 book, *After the Hangover: The Conservatives' Road to Recovery*, I explained, about as well as I can, why I capitalize the words *Liberal* and *Liberalism*. There I said that moribund Liberalism—and it *was* visibly dying by 2010—had to be distinguished, for clarity's sake, from true liberalism: classical liberalism or, as it is sometimes called, nineteenth-century liberalism.

Classical liberalism stood for adherence to individual liberty, to tolerance, to reason, and, for many of us, to empiricism. The Liberals through the decades had twisted all these values into absurdities. The vast majority of American conservatives are classic liberals, as George Washington was and Benjamin Franklin and all of the Founding Fathers. But to argue this point when Liberals were dominant in the culture was futile. Now, however, the Liberal mobs have subsided. Liberalism is dead. It died in the years preceding *Hangover*'s publication. I like to think the book hastened the conservatives' recovery. There are, admittedly, Liberal zombies still around. These living dead will continue their suicide missions, but I think even their end is near. How can they spend and spend, and tax and tax, when taxation is useless against the mounting debt? This country is a vibrant democracy. The Founders set it up that way. Liberalism was based on false promises and ultimately parasitism, but Liberalism is dead.

In the book you are about to read, you will undoubtedly become aware that I capitalize *Liberal* and *Liberalism* even as I invariably capitalize the word *God*. Please do not let this confuse you. I do not make this typological adjustment in deference to the Liberals' age-old habit of asserting their divine attributes. Rather, it is out of my recognition that the recently deceased Liberals were never liberal. Consequently, I want to distinguish Liberalism from the earlier liberalism, the aforementioned classical liberals or nineteenth-century liberals—for instance, me, and probably, you.

The recently deceased Liberals were so distinct from earlier liberals that I am not even certain there is an ancestral link. DNA samples are not readily available, but if they were, I believe that, say, the late Senator Edward Kennedy's claim to an ancestral relationship with, say, James Madison or Thomas Jefferson would be dismissed as illegitimate. Rather, it is we conservatives who can rightly claim ancestry reaching back to the Founding Fathers and beyond to Locke. Moreover, we need not go through the invasive process of procuring DNA samples. We can make our genealogical claim on the basis of shared principles, particularly our shared scruples about Big Government's threats to individual liberty and our shared enthusiasm for constitutionally limited government, the rule of law, and free markets that spread prosperity and preserve freedom. We are waging our own war on poverty. It is called "spreading prosperity," and it now spreads even abroad without coercion. Also like the Founding Fathers, we believe America is a blessed and exceptional nation.

Liberals in their last stages were collectivists. Some were stealth socialists. Others, the complete fools, teased us with their socialism. Remember the triumphal *Newsweek* headline of February 7, 2009: "We Are All Socialists Now"? The equivalents of these stealth socialists found elsewhere in the world are socialists, though very few are sufficiently oblivious of the dreary socialist reality to admit to the designation. Even in times of economic uncertainty, socialism remains very much out of fashion. Doubtless you noticed the Liberals' indignant howls when they were accused of socialism for nationalizing large portions of the private sector or for imposing a nanny state on private citizens. They shunned the term. Yet even as death embraced them, they championed unprecedented peacetime government controls. If the Obama administration proposed high-minded regulations for the bristles in your toothbrush or a safety-grip handle for it, you should not have been surprised. Properly understood, that is not very liberal. Consequently, to avoid confusion between the recently deceased Liberals and true liberals, I employ a capital *L*. Call it the scarlet letter.

A true liberal of the classic variety, Sir William Harcourt, made my point with elegance back in 1873 when he told a gathering at Oxford that

> liberty does not consist in making others do what you think is right. The difference between a free Government and a Government which is not free is principally this— that a Government which is not free interferes with everything it can, and a free Government interferes with nothing except what it must. A despotic government tries to make everybody do what it wishes, a Liberal Government tries, so far as the safety of society will permit, to allow everybody to do what he wishes."[1]

Let me hasten to add that my deployment of the capital *L* is not original. William F. Buckley Jr. and his editors at the *National Review* devised this expediency at the dawn of the modern conservative movement in the 1950s. As Buckley explained in the introduction to his 1959 book, *Up from Liberalism*, "I capitalize the words 'Liberal' and 'Liberalism,' by which I intend a pious gesture of historical deference to words (liberal, liberalism) that once meant something very different from what they have come to mean in contemporary American politics."[2] Yes, he joked, "pious gesture."

From his earliest days in journalism, Bill employed humor and wit in his political commentary and polemics. The practice has continued among prominent conservative writers up to the present, thus giving humor and wit a bad odor with Liberals in their last days and, I believe, explaining why their own commentary was usually devoid of these agreeable qualities. Surely at some level they must have known that at least *some* political activity was a hoot. Say, Bill Clinton's antics with that fat intern, or Barack Obama relying on a Teleprompter to greet schoolchildren. Well, perhaps not; Liberal politics seemed often to be motivated by what members of the American Psychiatric Association diagnose as free-floating anxiety or general anxiety disorder (GAD).

Possibly this explains the Liberals' creation in the late 1940s or early 1950s of another phenomenon that you will encounter in this book. I designated it some years ago as *Kultursmog*. The term has gained acceptance among objective observers such as Tom Wolfe, except that he calls it "the social manipulation of 'the Good,' a subset of the sociology of concept construction," and dates it back to the Phoenicians in the fifth century BC. Viewed from a more recent perspective, *Kultursmog* is the pollution of our culture by politics, almost exclusively Liberal politics. The Liberals' insistence on arrogating the word *liberal* despite their being the opposite of liberal is by now a commonplace example of *Kultursmog*. Later in this book I shall elaborate on the nature and noxious particulates of *Kultursmog*. For now, however, let me say that it is the only environmental hazard that remains untreated by government and unremarked by environmentalists—who themselves were leading contributors to the *smog*.

An historic revelation as to how the *Kultursmog* is made occurred late in 2009 when hackers broke into the electronic files of one of the world's leading Global Warmist research centers, the Climatic Research Unit (CRU) of the University of East Anglia in the United Kingdom, and posted some 3,000 of the Warmists' conspiratorial e-mails and files for all the world to read. To my ineffable gratification, the e-mails displayed the Global Warmists sedulously engaging in just what you would expect in the *Kultursmog*: deceits, distortions, and the suppression of dissenting points of view.

Now exposed on the Internet, adherents to the *Kultursmog*'s credo on Global Warming could be seen surreptitiously blacklisting and suppressing scientists who disagreed with them, the so-called "Global Warming skeptics." In one instance Michael Mann, director of the Earth System Science Center at Pennsylvania State University, e-mailed like-minded Global Warmists, advising them to isolate and ignore scientists and scientific journals that publish the views of the "skeptics." "I think we have to stop considering *Climate Research* as a legitimate peer-reviewed journal," he wrote, going on to urge the encouragement of "our colleagues in the climate research community to no longer submit to, or cite papers in, this journal." Now, that is precisely how *Kultursmog* taints the debate.

Then there was Phil Jones, director of the University of East Anglia project. He e-mailed Mr. Mann and others, adjuring them to "delete any emails you may have had with Keith" regarding indelicate references to the UN's Intergovernmental Panel on Climate Change's Fourth Assessment Report. Another e-mail from Jones to a coconspirator asked that he "change the Received date! Don't give those skeptics something to amuse themselves with." Also among the hacked e-mails was one from an unnamed scientist, urging his readers to "hide the decline" of temperatures in data that might indicate global cooling rather than Global Warming. His concern was understandable. At the time there had been no Global Warming for almost a decade, contrary to the Global Warmists' computer predictions. In fact, from 2005 until the Global Warmists' e-mail conspiracy was exposed, there had been Global Cooling!

Thanks to the work of these public-spirited hackers, the world has been given abundant evidence that the Global

Warmists are dishonest bullies. As for me, I have been given a perfect educational model to demonstrate how my discovery, *Kultursmog*, works. But this exposé is not without its melancholy aspects too. There once was a day when scientists were empiricists, believing in reason and fair play. Empiricism, reason, and fair play, of course, are some of the values observed by the original liberals and ignored by the Liberals of the recent past and by the zombies today.

RET
September 11, 2011
Old Town
Alexandria, Virginia

1

LIBERALISM IS DEAD: AN AUTOPSY OF THE MOVEMENT

In the tumultuous history of postwar American Liberalism, there has been a slow but steady decline of which the Liberals have been steadfastly oblivious. This pose has required admirable discipline, for the evidence was all around them. Yet Liberals, who began as the rightful heirs to the New Deal, have carried on as a kind of landed aristocracy, gifted but doomed. They dominated the culture and the politics of the country, unchallenged from the beginnings of the Cold War to the first Nixon administration. So dominant were they that they could totally pollute the culture with their prejudices and their views. In its place they created *Kultursmog*, a *Kultur* whose contaminants were everywhere: in the media, among the literate classes, even among illiterates—everywhere. *Kultursmog* is the only form of pollution to which the Liberals never object. In fact, they deem it healthy.

With the general populace, however, they have increasingly faltered, and now even in the *Kultur* they are making heavy weather of it. They are down to around 20 percent of the electorate. They have the nation's librarians, most of the professoriate—at least in the humanities—students (so long as they remain relatively untaxed), labor union leaders, and career Democrats. After that it gets tricky. Conservatives accounted for 42 percent of the vote in the recent election, maintaining a roughly two-to-one margin over Liberals, a superiority that has been growing for decades. In the last election the moderates—the second most popular affiliation—voted with conservatives. They were alarmed about the economy and will probably remain alarmed for a long time.

Liberals are going the way of the American Prohibition Party or the Know-Nothing Party. It is time for someone to tell them: "Rigor mortis has set in, comrades." They could be oblivious during the Nixon Crisis in 1973 and 1974 or while Ronald Reagan, as many Liberals still say, sleepwalked through history; but today their obliviousness amounts to a kind of madness. Their mansion is afire, but there is a whole string ensemble whose members are madly playing their instruments. As if all were well.

At first glance, the decline might appear to have begun with the 1961 inauguration of President John F. Kennedy when historians noted the first sightings of what was to become Liberalism's distinctive trait: overreach. At times Liberals promise too much. At times they attempt too much. Occasionally they actually achieve too much, leaving many Americans fearing for their liberties and the contents of their wallets. As a consequence, larger numbers of the electorate have been voting for conservatism, a movement that began in the 1950s when anticommunists combined with proponents of limited government and with advocates of traditional American values. For years it was a small, struggling movement, challenging Liberalism intellectually, but then Richard Nixon availed himself of parts of it. Nixon was too much the pol to be a movement conservative, but he saw the conservative movement's value. Then in the 1970s the movement became an intellectual and electoral force, and with the presidency of Ronald Reagan, it became the dominant force in American politics. The Liberals remained oblivious.

Kennedy's soaring oratory frequently attained the sublime meaninglessness of romantic poesy. It was lovely, but it roused the Soviets, led to the Vietnam quagmire, and put America in the role of defender of democracy to the world, not leaving us with much room to maneuver. It was, in truth, an extension of President Franklin D. Roosevelt's Four Freedoms. Even further back, it echoed President Woodrow Wilson's Fourteen Points. It was infectious and admirable, and it even impressed later generations of conservatives; but it was susceptible to overreach, and of course, it was a bit dishonest. For instance, there never was a missile gap, as Kennedy claimed, or any other cause for his histrionics. Moreover, on the domestic side, the oratory set in motion what was to be catastrophic overreach, President Lyndon Johnson's War on Poverty.

In a way JFK's stirring language represented a break with the Burkean understanding of President Dwight Eisenhower. Ike, whether he articulated it or not, wanted to put the Great Depression and the dangerous confrontations of the early Cold War behind us. He wanted to return to "normalcy." Yet JFK departed from Ike's more prudent course when he said in his first inaugural address, "Let every nation know, whether it wishes us well or ill, that we shall pay any price, bear any burden, meet any hardship, support any friend, oppose any foe to assure the survival and the success of liberty." He kept up the rhetorical barrage. Then on April 12, 1961, the Soviets sent Yuri Gagarin into space. A week later Kennedy betrayed ambivalence at the Bay of Pigs and immaturity at his June summit with the Soviet leader Nikita Khrushchev, who told his aides that by comparison Ike "was a man of intelligence and vision."[1] So he was.

Kennedy was inert as the East Germans walled off Berlin in August, and only reacted vigorously when he had the Cuban Missile Crisis on his hands in the autumn of 1962. Then the Great Blah began, with Richard Rovere writing in the *New Yorker* that the showman in the White House had achieved "perhaps the greatest personal diplomatic victory of any president in our history."[2] Oh, come on! Now the Soviets were roused, and America was on a path much more perilous than that which Ike had envisioned. It led to some of the tensest moments of the Cold War and on to war in Vietnam. It fixed America's stance in the world as defender of democracy. It led to the inevitability of war in Iraq and Afghanistan. Domestically it set us on the path to a behemoth Big Government.

Still, in looking for Liberalism's decline, the historian's eye falls on an earlier event as a precursor to Liberalism's present entombment: the civil war that broke out in the aftermath of World War II between what we might call the radical Liberals led by Henry Wallace and the more practical and tough-minded Liberals of whom Arthur M. Schlesinger Jr. sang in his 1949 book, *The Vital Center*. They were leaders like Hubert Humphrey in politics, the civil rights lawyer Joseph L. Rauh, and the labor leader Walter Reuther. They were hardheaded and patriotic, and the desiderata for their constituents were reasonable by comparison with the radicals' wild ideas.

Yet, even here in the late 1940s, they introduced the excesses that were to grow much worse. They instilled their Liberalism with a disturbing moralism and, even worse, the first Big Lie of modern American politics. Others would come—for instance, the allegation that anyone who questions their most recent panacea for race relations is a racist.

Or that anyone questioning their latest scheme of alleviating poverty hates the poor. Or—more recently—that Bill Clinton was a martyr of nigh unto virginal purity. When, as president of the United States, he lied under oath about his relations with Monica Lewinsky, the Liberals insisted that it was a minor infraction of the law, like double-parking one's tractor in downtown Little Rock.

The first Big Lie was that Alger Hiss, Harry Dexter White, and other security risks were not Communists. We now know with the opening of the Venona files that they were. Intelligence officers conducting the Venona project surely conveyed their knowledge to political leaders. Yet Secretary of State James F. Byrnes and fellow Democrats, like Dean Acheson, for various reasons, did not think the truth mattered. Hiss and his kind were eccentrics or idealists. By 1948 what mattered was keeping the dreaded Republicans out of government. Maybe they were right that Hiss's Communism was a harmless thing, but they did not have to lie about it. The Hiss debate brought discredit to Liberalism and has envenomed our politics right up to the present.

The practical Liberals won in the late 1940s, but in 1972 civil war broke out anew. This time the radicals won with the Democratic nomination of Senator George McGovern for president. The radicals had changed the rules of the Democratic Party, thus ensuring their victories in subsequent conventions. Simultaneously with this radical takeover of the Democratic Party, radicals took over the universities, bringing in nonsense studies and idiot enthusiasms. In the meantime, LBJ's Great Society was an egregious instance of overreach, causing even some Liberals to warn against the "unintended consequences" of government programs. These straying Liberals were to be the first new recruits to modern conservatism, which was now growing fast. The radicals' conquests of the Democratic Party and of the universities hastened the straying Liberals' journey to conservatism. Such Liberals as Jeane Kirkpatrick, Irving Kristol, Norman Podhoretz, and for a time, Daniel Patrick Moynihan, were in Kristol's words Liberals "who were mugged by reality."[*]

At the same time, the radical Liberals became more self-indulgent. They were of two types: the aging students who had in the late 1960s been called Coat-and-Tie Radicals and the more serious ideologues. The first grew up to become Infantile Leftists. The second either were or became socialists, though they dared not use the word—even Social Democrat was out. Only a crisis in the leadership of President Nixon allowed the general electorate to ignore these transformations.

---

[*] Erased from history, probably by the *Kultursmog*, was precisely how close Pat was to the conservatives, especially to *The American Spectator*. Late in 1977, when our first publisher, John Von Kannon, came down with cancer, the junior senator from New York, Pat Moynihan, called Von Kannon's Indianapolis hospital and promised him help with any experimental medication he might need. Pat was a pal.

How grave Nixon's misbehavior was in Watergate, I leave to history. I shall only say this: There is a formal and an informal politics. In the formal politics we play by the rules. In the informal politics we break the lesser rules from time to time. Everyone in Washington suspected, when informed of Watergate, that Nixon had suggested sotto voce to his lieutenants, "Rid me of this problem." LBJ had done it with such rogues as Bobby Baker. Truman had done it with numerous scoundrels, and FDR did it with a wide array, from Maurice Parmalee, a practicing nudist, to Jesse Jones, his secretary of commerce. Most modern Big Government presidents say, "I don't want to hear about it," and the thing is dealt with by others. Perhaps it was the surpassing moralism of modern Liberalism that would not allow the dispensation to hold in Nixon's case.

At any rate, the latest Washington truism became, "Worse than the lie is the cover-up." In the subsequent cleansing, much of Southeast Asia went Communist. It became dangerous to be numbered among America's friends. By now Liberalism was becoming lost in its fantasies. To the Liberal, conservatives became truly evil, while each Liberal became a moral colossus, a truth seeker, a poet. Possibly the first attempts at windsurfing were then undertaken and jogging around the Lincoln Memorial in one's underpants—more on this later. The Liberals began to confer with only the like-minded. They lost touch with America. They almost never establish communication with the American conservatives. David Mamet, the Pulitzer Prize–winning playwright, admits in his tale of conversion to conservatism, *The Secret Knowledge: On the Dismantling of American Culture*, that not until the age of sixty did he ever talk politics or anything else with a conservative. Quite possibly he never knowingly met one. When the Liberals were trounced by conservatives in 2010, they really never knew what hit them. They continued to practice denial.

Conservatives have had Edmund Burke, the Earl of Beaconsfield (Benjamin Disraeli), and the Founding Fathers as their cynosures. Sometimes they have provided conservatives with discipline and direction. Sometimes the conservatives have followed their own star. The problem for Liberals is they have been denied a cynosure. Some had looked to the British Fabians and some to Karl Marx, but since the late 1940s and the recognition of the Soviet Union's costs in liberty (and lives) and social democracy's costs to GDP, people like John Kenneth Galbraith became coy about their intellectual heroes. Some pointed to John Stuart Mill, but so did some conservatives. John Maynard Keynes was useful but too narrow. So the Liberals really have no formidable ancestors to claim—certainly no Burkes, not even a couple of the Founding Fathers. Maybe Jean-Jacques Rousseau or more recently Saul Alinsky, but the first is lost in his dithyrambs and the second probably stole hubcaps or maybe whole cars.

Actually, around the 1970s, one could hear scattered clarions of the moribund Liberalism claiming the Beatles as Liberal *philosophes*. After all, since the 1960s rock 'n' roll had a special place in the Liberals' weltanschauung. Sean Wilentz, the modern-day heir to Schlesinger, has even written a scholarly study of Bob Dylan. Did Schlesinger ever write a book about Frank Sinatra or, earlier, Glenn Miller? As I say, Liberalism is dead.

By the 1980s the leadership of the Liberal cause could be divided into two types, the Infantile Leftist and a smaller camp, the stealth socialists. The Infantile Leftist talked of global warming, some sort of government health care, and increasingly one world under one law—that sort of thing. They did not talk of socialism, but doubtless if the wind came up and filled out socialism's sails, they would gladly be swept along. The stealth socialists laid low until very recently, and even now they are not very candid, adopting a pose of "Read my deeds" rather than "Read my lips." In the glorious, if delusional, aftermath of the 2008 election, when revolution was in the air—at least for some—*Newsweek* jumped the gun with an idiotic piece by editor Jon Meacham, titled "We Are All Socialists Now: *In many ways our economy already resembles a European one. As boomers age and spending grows, we will become even more French*" (italics in the original).[3] But since then, even the stealth socialists have subsided. The looming costs of our socialist monstrosity have become a grim monument to fiscal extravagance.

The Infantile Left has provided me with a lot of laughs— for example, Al Gore's historic kiss at the 2000 Democratic Convention and Jean-François Kerry, the Vietnam war protester claiming to be the war hero. By contrast President Barack Obama, a stealth socialist if ever there was one, is not so funny, though occasionally he comes up with such derisible lines as "We are the ones we've been waiting for. We are the change that we seek."[4] There has been controversy over his authorship of various works, but I think he probably wrote that line himself.

From the Nixon administration on, the numbers have not been good for Liberals. In 1972 only one state went for George McGovern, and that was not even his home state. He even lost the youth vote, though one would never know it from reading the press accounts in the *Kultursmog*. The belief that youth is always with the Liberal candidate is one of Liberalism's marmoreal myths. In 1976 Liberalism did better, but Jimmy Carter ran as a moderate, and God gave him Watergate. Then came 1980. Reagan benefited from the ongoing electoral accretions that modern conservatism had attracted: the Neoconservatives, the evangelicals (aka the Christian Right), and the Reagan Democrats. The

Liberals could only claim blacks, feminists, some gays, and some Latinos. In other words, nothing new—just perpetrators of what we call "masked politics." When the masks slipped, one could see that they all had been Liberals all along, Liberals for whom Liberalism had become, in the words of the longshoreman philosopher Eric Hoffer, "a racket."[5] During the eight years of the Reagan administration, Reagan changed the political center for years to come. His conservative policies worked. As the Old Cowboy headed back to California, the political center was center-right: vigilance about Big Government; balanced budgets, low taxes, and peace through strength.

In 1992, after twelve years of conservatives in the White House, Bill Clinton beat a peculiarly weak George H. W. Bush. Bush had an 89 percent approval rating (8 percent disapproval rating) the year before his defeat, according to the Gallup poll. Surely the third-party candidacy of Ross Perot and general conservative dissatisfaction with Bush took a toll. At any rate, Clinton, like Carter, ran as a moderate. Once in office, he initially tried to push a Liberal Big Government agenda with an infrastructure buildup and health care reform. He was thrashed in the midterm election, losing both chambers, and the House of Representatives by the biggest shift since 1948. The rest of Clinton's presidency followed the conversion that he himself proclaimed, "The era of Big Government is over." The Reagan Revolution was secured. In 2000 Clinton's vice president, Al Gore, lost to the governor of Texas (and George H. W. Bush's son, George W. Bush), despite widespread prosperity and peace. President Bush won the midterms in 2002, increasing his margins in both houses, and in 2004 he won a second term.

Then came the Republicans' Wilderness Years in 2006 and 2008—but not conservatism's. Its adherents were still far more numerous than those of Liberalism. Conservatism has steadily spread throughout the Republic since its larval days in the 1950s, and Liberalism has declined to its present need for a proper burial.

The reason is that the vast majority of Americans favor free enterprise and personal liberty. Arthur Brooks of the American Enterprise Institute, in his book, *The Battle*, offers a figure that roughly approximates other studies: 70 percent of Americans who favor free enterprise and personal liberty versus 30 percent of Americans who do not favor such freedom. In 2010, the Republicans took the House of Representatives by 63 seats and gained 6 seats in the Senate, abetted by conservatism's latest recruits, supporters of the Tea Party movement. They added 715 legislative seats nationwide and 6 governorships. Democrats lost control of 20 state legislatures. The Stealth Socialist in the White House (the term originated with Obama's definitive biographer, Stanley Kurtz) was denied his majority by a rout. Fully 42 percent of the electorate is conservative. Of the 29 percent that is moderate, 56 percent went with the Republicans in this election, nudged by the economy and jobs. Liberals account for 20 percent of the vote. This spread has pretty much endured for thirty years with the moderate vote alternately diminishing and swelling the conservatives' vote.

Think of that when you recall all those obituarists writing about the death of conservatism but two years before. What is more, consider this anecdote: Months after the 2010 election, one could saunter into one of Liberalism's holy shrines, the Washington, D.C., bookshop Politics & Prose. There, one could still see bravely displayed out in the open Sam Tanenhaus's suicidal 2009 book, *The Death of Conservatism.* Devout Liberals might light little votive lights before it. At the time, I bought my copy from Amazon for nineteen cents.

In the two years after the 2008 election, the Democrats showed their true colors. Faced with an entitlement crisis, they actually rang up additional trillion-dollar deficits. We now face the entitlement crisis *and* a budget crisis, and the Liberals have no answer for either beyond tax and spend. They still have support in the media, but even here they are faced with opposition from Fox News, talk radio, and the Internet. The *Kultursmog* is finally beginning to disperse. Even the Europeans are facing up to the cost of the welfare state, but the Liberals can only spend and tax, though their taxes appear futile against our towering debt.

As a political movement, Liberalism is dead. Its acolytes do not have the numbers. They do not have the policies. They have 23 seats in the Senate to defend in 2012 (against the Republicans' 10), and increased Republican control of governorships and legislatures will possibly give Republicans even more seats in the House of Representatives in the future. Liberalism, R.I.P. Even Liberals do not call themselves Liberal today. They identify themselves as Progressives. It fools no one.

2

LIBERALISM IN AMERICA

Now, when we talk about the death of Liberalism, we are talking about the contemporary species of the animal—for instance, the soi-disant Liberal Lion of the Senate, Teddy Kennedy, who, incidentally, really *is* dead. We are not talking about Hubert Humphrey or Adlai Stevenson or their supporting cast of intellectuals such as Walter Lippmann or Arthur M. Schlesinger Jr. or John Kenneth Galbraith. We are talking about lesser specimens, Kennedy, George McGovern, and most recently the Hon. Nancy Pelosi and, of course, the Hon. Barney Frank. Also we are talking about their intellectual accompaniment, but a careful investigation shows that there is no intellectual accompaniment. There are presumptuous Hollywoodians and obscure professors usually to be found in women's studies or Black studies or some other ethnic indulgence, but that is about it. I shall endeavor to explain this void in chapter 7.

Before Kennedy assumed room temperature, he was emblematic of what we are dealing with today. In fact, he was quite possibly the best of the breed. Notwithstanding his scurrilous attack on Judge Robert Bork*—now understood to have been wildly inaccurate—and other lesser defamations of conservatives who roused his partisan juices, he was a forceful advocate for various programs on the Liberal agenda that, though unworkable and often lavishly expensive, were based on some sort of intellectual scaffolding: socialized medicine, gun control, or colluding with the Soviets in thwarting the hellish Reagan from putting intermediate range missiles in Europe—and there was a goofball coda to this story. While colluding with Moscow to scotch the warmonger Reagan, Teddy hoped that his new allies would help him gain the presidency in 1984 from poor old Ronald Reagan.**

Teddy drank a lot in those days.

---

* Of Bork he memorably declaimed on the Senate floor, "Robert Bork's America is a land in which women would be forced into back-alley abortions, blacks would sit at segregated lunch counters, rogue police would break down citizens' doors in midnight raids, school children could not be taught about evolution, writers and artists could be censored at the whim of government, and the doors of federal courts would be shut on the fingers of millions of citizens." All are charges utterly without factual basis but were taken by his supporters as gospel, which is another indication that even in 1987, the year the charges were made, Liberalism, as an act of ratiocination, was dead.

** The amazing misadventure was reported in the February 2, 1992, *London Times* under the headline "Teddy, the KGB and the top secret file" and went pretty much unremarked in America until Paul Kengor reported Teddy's correspondence and presidential aspirations in his 2006 book, *The Crusader: Ronald Reagan and the Fall of Communism*, though in the *Kultursmog* it is ignored.

Yet through it all he had a habit of going off on sprees with Liberal colleagues like Senator Christopher Dodd. One of their favorite Washington haunts was La Colline, where they would get thoroughly plastered, break crockery, and tear down pictures of their senatorial colleagues from the walls. Another was La Brasserie, where they would occasionally rough up a woman, and Teddy might be caught girl-hopping with his pants off.[1] Occasionally he would journey afar. For instance, the FBI reports that the year before joining the Senate, Teddy attempted to rent out an entire whorehouse in Chile. Closer to home, he would journey to the wilds of Palm Beach with his nephews and a son for nocturnal outings. During one famed jaunt he paraded around, again with his pants off, while nephew William took a woman down to the beach and engaged in sex that she characterized as rape, leading to the nephew's indictment.[*]

In fact, Kennedy's career was marked by one mishap that a generation before would have ended any politician's career, either voluntarily or involuntarily. Looking back on it now, it appears as a historic moment in the decline of Liberalism: Chappaquiddick. On that boozy occasion he left a young aide from brother Bob's presidential campaign, Mary Jo Kopechne, to fend for herself in

---

[*] He was eventually acquitted, but not before three other women came forward claiming victimization by him.

a submerged Oldsmobile while he swam across the bay, crawled into bed, and after sleeping fretfully, began calling his servitors to counsel him on how best to protect his career. Miss Kopechne drowned.[2]

Kennedy survived Chappaquiddick, and though he never became president,[3] he did persevere to become, as the *Kultursmog* had it, the Lion of the Senate. It was a comeback that was to be duplicated by a rising generation of Liberal roués with such frequency that historians will someday note that a seminal point was arrived at in the decline of Liberalism when Liberals were suddenly capable of surviving what in any prior era would be a career-ending scandal. Call it the Chappaquiddick Dispensation. The *Kultursmog*'s role helped. In fact, the *smog* was almost complicit.

The Rev. Jesse Jackson survived at least two such scandals. In the first, he spoke colorfully of New York City as "Hymietown" to a *Washington Post* reporter. Hymietown, however, was not his only anti-Semitic reference. The interview was sprinkled with many other highly imaginative anti-Semitic references revealing him as a seasoned bigot.[4]

In a second scandal, he was caught paying off a pregnant mistress with the tax-deductible funds from charities he controlled—rather astonishingly he had brought her to the White House while he was counseling Bill Clinton on the Monica Lewinsky matter. It was counseling of a physiological and moral nature. His mistress was four months pregnant![5] They *posed* for White House pictures! His transgressions were as nothing when compared with those of the Rev. Al Sharpton, who went on to become a respected Democratic adviser and TV personality. More recently he has become an occasional adviser to President Barack Obama despite his involvement twenty years before in at least two anti-Semitic incidents in Brooklyn Heights and in Harlem that left eight people dead and buildings razed. These tragic events followed his clownish 1987 advocacy of Tawana Brawley's preposterous allegations of rape by white assailants, a discredited charge that nonetheless heightened racial tensions while making Sharpton famous. Before the Chappaquiddick Dispensation, Sharpton's career in public life, too, would have ended, certainly by the time of the Brawley affair.

Which brings us to the contemporary Liberals who prevailed over a whole string of scandals that in any other era would have ended their careers, thus sparing the nation what became, for those of us who could still laugh, the Clinton's Cavalcade of Revelry. I refer to Bill Clinton and his lovely wife, Bruno. Both Bill and Hillary lied before grand juries, engaged in repeated fund-raising scams as far back as Arkansas, and inspired so many "____gates" that even I tired of the suffix. It all ended in Pardon*gate*, which involved 140 impudent pardons along with 36 commutations, with numerous payoffs being made to their loutish brothers, one of whom, Roger Clinton, was himself a convicted drug offender. The Clintons' saga should have ended years before we ever met Monica or were dragged through the spectacle of Bill's impeachment. Yet in accordance with the Chappaquiddick Dispensation, he survived the early scandals, and even Pardongate at the very end of his presidency was mere ephemera.

On that occasion we saw another milestone in Liberalism's historic demise, to wit, public denunciations by a scandal-plagued Liberal that were soon lost in memory's well. No Liberal before Pardongate received so many weighty rebukes from his colleagues, only to emerge in a matter of years, repristinated. Savor these estimates of the forty-second president upon his absconding from the White House. Clinton was "totally indefensible" (Joe Biden); "disgraceful" (Jimmy Carter); "terrible," "devastating," and "appalling" (William Daley); "Clinton is utterly disgraced" (former Clinton secretary of labor Robert Reich); and "some of Mr. Clinton's closest associates and supporters are acknowledging what his enemies have argued for years—the man is so thoroughly corrupt it is frightening" (*New York Times* columnist Bob Herbert).[6] I could continue, but you get my drift. All would, of course, be back aboard the Clintons' tawdry bandwagon by 2003 and in agreement with John F. Harris's assessment of the Clintons. In his 2005 book, *The Survivor: Bill Clinton in the White House*, Harris made the stupefying judgment that the Clintons are "the two most important political figures of their generation."[7] Now, one may not approve of George W. Bush and Newt Gingrich, but they were rather important political figures, and they were in the Clintons' generation. Bush got us into a war.

Two editorials also stand out as illustrative of the Liberals' peculiar state of mind during Liberalism's last days. The *New York Times* called for Congressional investigations of the ex–Boy President, lamenting that "the former president . . . seemed to make a redoubled effort in the last moments of his presidency to plunge further and further beneath the already low expectations of his most cynical critics and most world-weary friends."[8] The *New York Observer* noted that the Clintons' critics "were right, after all. Mr. Clinton was, in fact, an untrustworthy low-life who used people for his own purposes and then discarded them."[9] As for Hillary, the newspaper charged that New Yorkers had "made a terrible mistake, for Hillary Rodham Clinton is unfit for elective office. Had she any shame, she would resign."[10] In a matter of years, both Clintons were back in the good graces of the *Kultursmog*, and the *smog* was doing its best to help us forget their indiscretions. By then the *Times* was booming Hillary for president, and MSNBC eventually would be airing "President of the World: The Clinton Phenomenon."[11] Bill had already been mentioned prominently for UN secretary general.

There were others who escaped the consequences of colossal scandal: the low-life governor of New York Eliot Spitzer, who terrorized legitimate businessmen only to be nabbed as "Client 9" in a very toney prostitution ring. He, too, was exempted from a life lived in exile, and after a short spell, perhaps in therapy, he began appearing on television, actually landing his own show on CNN. Most surprisingly, it had nothing to do with sexual hygiene.

Then there was the derisible Senator Jean-François Kerry, who made his fortune marrying not one but two rich women, the second of whom derived her wealth from marriage to a rich man, a Republican senator, John Heinz. Senator Kerry was the Democrats' standard-bearer in 2004, and he opted to run as a war hero despite the existence of his taped 1971 testimony before Congress that would prove very damaging to him, though he was himself quite oblivious. There on tape he can be seen charging fellow soldiers—*and possibly himself*—with war crimes.[12] The newly transformed peacenik, though still a naval officer, had even journeyed to France to enter into some sort of confabulation with the Vietnamese Communists, an act that could have earned him the charge of treason or at least a less-than-honorable discharge from the Navy. In fact, it might have. There has always been a cloud of murk surrounding his military record. Nonetheless, he presumed to run for the presidency in 2004 as a hero and was astonished when some of his former buddies from Vietnam formed the Swift Boat Veterans for Truth to protest his delusional war. At least he lost, but he bamboozled a lot of Democrats, and "Swift Boating" became accepted in the *Kultursmog* as a term comparable to knifing a war hero in the back.

The delusional hero's running mate was Senator John Edwards, whose own career may be historic. He may represent the end of the line for the Chappaquiddick Dispensation. Possibly there will be no more Liberals riding out what, in another age, would have meant professional suicide. During his own run for the presidency in 2008, he impregnated a campaign advisor even as his wife was fighting terminal cancer, which he naturally enough was exploiting for all it was worth. What is more, Edwards attempted to have a campaign aide claim paternity for the child while Edwards financed the bogus ménage from his campaign funds—quite illegal. When the entire scheme blew up, he not only had to bow out of the race, but he also faced indictment with not even a slot on CNN awaiting him. By 2008 Americans had possibly had enough. In 2011, when Congressman Anthony Weiner—a famed Democrat scold—was caught sending lewd pictures of his best friend (his erect penis) to women he hardly knew, he tried to brazen it out and remain in Congress. He was borrowing a play from the Clinton presidential playbook. He even had one of

Hillary's aides for his wife. She was pregnant! Nonetheless, he was drummed from office by his Democratic colleagues. Possibly the Chappaquiddick Dispensation is defunct.

Still, the number of reprobates allowed careers on the national stage in Liberalism's last days is amazing, and by contrast no conservative was ever capable of sweating through a scandal of any kind. Did South Carolina's Romeo governor Mark Sanford go on to better things? During the era of Liberal invulnerability to scandal, a dozen or more conservatives smelling of perfume that was not their wives' shuffled off to early retirement.[13] It was clearly a double standard. Still, a double standard is better than no standard at all. Let us all be grateful that at least one party is held accountable in the *smog.* Of the Republicans, only Newt Gingrich showed any chance of a political reactivation after a scandal, and he has been so piteously mauled and weakened in the *Kultursmog* that it has yet to be demonstrated that he will be president of the United States, much less a candidate for either of the happy job openings imagined for Bill Clinton.

Of course, there are automatons from Liberalism's last days out there still capable of spending a trillion here, a trillion there, from the United States Treasury. Nancy Pelosi may have run in 2006 promising that "Democrats are committed to no deficit spending, pay-as-you-go. We will not heap mountains of debt onto future generations."[14] As Speaker of the House, however, she was unrestrained by that declamation and was wildly profligate, spending vast sums of money and lavishing even more after Barack Obama was elected in 2008.

Like zombies, she and her Democratic colleagues from the left of the spectrum will be staggering on in 2012 and 2014, mouthing the slogans of yesteryear. Conservatives will have to pick off these living dead as they can. I do not mean to say that the Liberal zombies cannot still do harm. They will *whoop-whoop* about the rich and the racists as long as the Liberals are out on the street, but they will come up with no new ideas and probably no new racists.

If given a chance, they will spend trillions and raise taxes everywhere, but they have no way to retire the debt they build up. Even though they might expropriate the billionaires and tax the millionaires into middle-class socio-economic discomfort, the debt will still be crushing. Withal, the conservatives and the independents are wise to them. Both groups are aware of the huge budgetary overhang facing government at every level, and that is a sobering per-spective. They have seen the Liberals *en flagrante*, and they recognize the futility of electing them again. The zombies must be monitored and finished off one at a time. Some zombies, like the bitter-end Roosevelt haters of yesteryear, will simply have to die off. There is no reasoning with them.

You might well ask, where did the taxers and spend-ers and social engineers come from? Were they always so egregious? Actually the contemporary Liberals are the last, rather pathetic, often buffoonish, evolutionary spin-offs of an audacious creature from the late nineteenth century, known as the Progressive. The early Progressives were at first plausible, even useful, but they evanesced, by the 1920s, to be replaced by the Harding administration led by secretary of the Treasury Andrew Mellon and later by "Silent Cal" Coolidge.

John Maynard Keynes, a distant British relative of the American Progressives, famously said, "When the facts change, I change my mind. What do you do, sir?" The contemporary Liberals living out their days in the early twenty-first century apparently never noticed that the facts had changed. They were seized by manias: for instance, the mania for high-speed rail service, thinking the "bullet trains" were the modern equivalent of the New Deal's power projects such as the Hoover Dam or the Tennessee Valley Authority. At times they simply gave themselves over to fits of anger like so many mad dogs barking at the moon. There was Senator Richard Durbin on the floor of the Senate, shouting, "If I read this to you and did not tell you it was an FBI agent describing what Americans had done to prisoners in their control, you would most certainly believe this must have been done by Nazis, Soviets in their gulags, or some mad regime—Pol Pot or others—that had no concern for human beings."[15] He was talking about U.S.

soldiers' alleged treatment of prisoners at Guantánamo. Or there was Senator Harry Reid in 2007, whimpering, "This war is lost and the surge is not accomplishing anything as indicated by the extreme violence in Iraq yesterday."[16]

In the late nineteenth century and the first two decades of the twentieth century, troubled by the excesses of the Industrial Revolution and by the radically changed landscape of America, the Progressives clamored forth with apprehensions, some of which are still with us, and certitudes, some of which now have been filed away as unseemly: for instance, eugenics, well-intentioned racism, and on a lighter note, phrenology—a well-shaped head signifying a well-shaped soul. The Progressives thought themselves very modern, and I guess they were, though they did not superannuate all the knowledge of the past. To the Progressives, the Founding Fathers had a musty air about them. They had created our constitutional system a century before, but that was in an era of horse-drawn carriages and powdered wigs, much as Aristotle is from the distant centuries, when philosophers dressed in bedsheets. You would not expect a self-respecting Progressive to dress in a bedsheet or wear a powdered wig.

A wide array of thinkers enlisted in the Progressive cause, from the novelist Upton Sinclair to the architect Frank Lloyd Wright to the historian Charles Beard. The most systematic Progressives were thinkers like Herbert Croly, founder of the *New Republic*; Charles Merriam; and the educator John Dewey. Their political leaders were often powerful men. Two were presidents, Theodore Roosevelt and Woodrow Wilson.

Wilson bespoke the Progressives' impatience with the Founding Fathers when he wrote: "All that progressives ask or desire is permission—in an era when 'development,' 'evolution,' is the scientific word—to interpret the constitution according to the Darwinian principle; all they ask is recognition of the fact that a nation is a living thing and not a machine."[17] Truth be known, the Founding Fathers never conceived of the nation as a machine. I am not sure who did. The Founders believed that human nature was divided, capable of good or evil. They thought freedom was part of human nature, allowing us to choose good or evil. That is why they tasked government to protect freedom, through checks and balances, the separation of powers—a system that, as *The Federalist* Number 10 proclaimed, allowed competing interests to wrangle and to vie with each other. Thus the tyranny of the majority would be thwarted, and abuse of government power made difficult.

The Progressives were unshakable believers in progress, about which contemporary Liberals are squeamish. Continued exploration of outer space makes them anxious. Nuclear energy, or for that matter, any energy not available from the sun or a passing breeze, leaves them almost hysterical. Progressives believed that great advances had been made in morals and in the scientific understanding of society. They believed that those who understood these advances could apply them to everything from government to the modernization of language to city planning, even to gardening. Checks and balances were antiquated. They were nuisances hindering these bright fellows from affixing onto society the most advanced ways to educate, medicate, nourish, and otherwise improve the lunkheads.

The Progressives were democrats, and they favored the *demos*, but the *demos* needed a proper education. The Progressives had a sense of confidence and of superiority about them, but it often bloomed into arrogance and moralism, at times rather breathtaking moralism. That quality has endured all through the generations of Liberalism. In fact, Liberals in their last stages have been afflicted by a free-floating moralism that makes it very difficult to approach them with alternative propositions. Advances in the way we live as diverse as the Internet and modern commerce have become vexed moral issues for many Liberals. The first they want to tax. The second they want to regulate, then tax.

As Peter Berkowitz of the Hoover Institution has ironically written, "The Constitution's obsolete and cumbersome institutional design was a primary hindrance to democratic reforms to which all reasonable people could agree and which upright and impartial administrators would implement."[18] Thinking like this led the Progressives to the easy conclusion that those who opposed them were "unreasonable" and benighted. They were tools of vested interests. Decades later, the opponents of the left were portrayed as contaminated by racism, male chauvinism, and worse. They were the agents of the Giant Corporations. Their arguments did not have to be taken seriously. At best, their arguments issue from a false consciousness, which is among Progressivism's inheritances from Karl Marx. The Progressives composed an elite stratum of society. Right up to the present day, as idiotic as it may sound, intellectual lightweights such as Al Gore—or more laughable still, Barbra Streisand—see themselves as numbered among the political elite. This way of approaching political disagreement is one of the Progressives' residual bequests to Liberalism on its deathbed. From its earliest days to its last, the American left has not had to take disagreement seriously. Those who disagreed with them they defined as unreasonable and a little thick in the cerebral cortex.

In 2010 the Liberals never engaged their opponents. Challengers were treated as a mob outside the Liberals' windows. Psychiatrists call this phenomenon *denial*, and the Liberals practiced denial even after the elections and into 2011. For a while it seemed that Speaker Pelosi would not give up her Speaker's gavel. Eventually she did, but the authorities were worried. She went quietly, but she never did acknowledge that she had lost the House.

The early Progressives were reacting to the enormous growth and change wrought by the Industrial Revolution and modern commercial enterprise. They were offended by monopolies and by the arbitrary exercise of power. Admirably, they wanted to protect the little guy, the exploited, the victimized, the wronged. They wanted democracy to work better. There was something refreshingly candid about them. They wanted to place themselves between the fat cats and the lunkheaded demos. Unlike contemporary Liberals, they admitted it.

As Croly wrote in his 1909 book, *The Promise of American Life*:

> To be sure, any increase in centralized power and responsibility, expedient or inexpedient, is injurious to certain aspects of traditional American democracy. But the fault in that case lies with the democratic tradition; and the erroneous and misleading tradition must yield before the march of a constructive national democracy. The national advance will always be impeded by these misleading and erroneous ideas, and, what is more, it always should be impeded by them, because at bottom ideas of this kind are merely an expression of the fact that *the average American individual is morally and intellectually inadequate to a serious and consistent conception of his responsibilities as a democrat.*[19]

Barack Obama rephrased the Progressives' understanding of disagreement in the body politic in 2008, bringing it into our time: "It's not surprising, then, they get bitter, they [those who disagree with contemporary Liberals] cling to guns or religion or antipathy to people who aren't like them, or anti-immigrant sentiment or anti-trade sentiment as a way to explain their frustration."[20] Of course, he was talking at a behind-closed-doors meeting with contributors. By 2008 you would never express these arrogant opinions in public.

3

LIBERALISM'S FIRST
CIVIL WAR, 1946–1948

There was always an abundance of crazy enthusiasts around Liberalism as well as men and women of moment; at least the men and women of moment were around until recent decades. The mixture gave Liberalism a kind of zany charm just as conservatism's reactionaries in years gone by gave conservatism a melancholy charm.

Doubtless, one of Liberalism's momentous women, certainly through the 1930s and up to the 1960s, was Eleanor Roosevelt. She was a tireless force for civil rights, for blacks, for women, for the down-and-out. She was always, however, subject to progressive thought's zanies. When her firstborn, Anna, came into the world, Eleanor was under the spell of the forward-leaning pediatrician L. Emmett Holt, a prestidigitator of, I think we can all agree today, some pretty fla fla views. He was an advocate of firm and rather eccentric child discipline starting at an early age. Little Anna's thumb sucking was to be arrested by tying her arms to her sides. Kissing was discouraged for fear of contracting diphtheria, tuberculosis, and venereal disease. A matter of the utmost importance in Dr. Holt's view was that an infant be "aired" for as long as five hours a day. Eleanor attempted this by putting the babe in a wooden box covered by chicken wire. This she suspended from her bedroom window until a neighbor threatened to call the Society for the Prevention of Cruelty to Children.[1] At age three, Anna had her hands tied to the top of her crib at night to prevent her from masturbating—strong evidence that, though Eleanor might have enjoyed the company of women, she was free of lesbianism's physical demands.[2]

Another Liberal figure of great moment in the 1930s and 1940s was Henry Wallace, who ended his days in the raucous hills and dales of the zanies. Wallace was FDR's second vice president. He was eased out with consummate cunning by the master in 1944 and replaced by Senator Harry S. Truman. Had Wallace remained vice president or had FDR died a year earlier, President Ronald Reagan's eventual achievement of ending the Cold War without firing a shot might have been tricky. As it was, Wallace settled in as Roosevelt's secretary of commerce, departing the administration in September of 1946 to become editor of the Liberal weekly, the *New Republic*. There he began what would be the first of Liberalism's two civil wars. In this first civil war, which lasted roughly from 1946 though 1948, Wallace led his dreamy-eyed "Gideon's Army," counseled and at times directed by Communist manipulators. They struggled against the Americans for Democratic Action (ADA), its suddenly tough-minded Liberals, and the Democrats' eventual presidential candidate in 1948, President Truman.

In generalizing about a movement of intellectuals, or political intellectuals, one always runs the hazard of having an outspoken member of the group pop up with a contradictory pronunciamento to cast doubt on one's generalizations. Michael Straight, publisher of the *New Republic*, was initially smitten by Wallace, only to quietly meld in with the tough-minded Liberals and, by 1949, actually undertake a speaking tour for the ADA. So there will be discordant voices, but basically my generalizations have been borne out by time. In the late 1940s this volatility was especially true, for it was a time of kaleidoscopic change in Liberalism. Truman, to name one, began 1947 leaning toward the "Wall Streeters." Soon he had instituted a loyalty program to ferret out Communists and their sympathizers in government. It was arguably a prelude to McCarthyism, and it made the Liberals edgy.

Still, by the second half of the year, Truman had adjusted his policies to mollify them, and the Liberals increasingly leaned toward Truman. Some did so reluctantly, but by late

1947 there was a growing number of anti-Wallace Liberals, and they had no place to go but to Truman, which they did with varying degrees of enthusiasm. Wallace's sentimental Popular Front sympathies had become intolerable. They were an embarrassment to the increasingly anticommunist Liberals. By now, fellow travelers had taken over the introverted leader's public pronouncements.

In part, a memo from Truman's young aide, Clark Clifford, governed the president's maneuvering. In it Clifford famously emphasized that the Liberals, while small in number compared to the labor unions or to the urban machines and lacking their obvious clout, had clout of their own, the "idea men." Very perceptively he wrote, "The 'right' may have the money, but the 'left' has always had the pen."[3] It was an acknowledgment of a condition that grew to become, by the late 1950s, the *Kultursmog*.

Liberalism's First Civil War began around 1946. By then the Liberals found themselves demoralized, fragmented, confused as to strategies, and without a leader. Roosevelt had died in April of 1945, leaving the unprepossessing Truman seemingly ill prepared to head the free world. The 1946 midterm elections were a dreadful setback for Liberals. Wallace was beginning to rip and snort, and anticommunism was becoming a looming issue for the country as a whole and especially for Liberals, who did not know what to do with Reds, whether domestic-born or Moscow-based. The Liberals sought an alternative to Truman but got nowhere. Times were tough.

Earlier Liberals had formed an alliance with the Popular Front against fascism, and fascism still alarmed them even with Hitler and Mussolini dead in Europe and no sign of fascism at home, certainly not to the untroubled eye. Thus in 1946 most Liberals did not want to do anything to disturb the Popular Fronters, who were always easily agitated. As 1947 came around, many Liberals did not know what to do when confronted with Truman's policy of Containment, the Truman Doctrine, or even something as benign as the Marshall Plan, which offered funding for the economic redevelopment of Europe, including the Soviet bloc before Moscow rejected it.

As the breakup of the victorious Big Three continued, most Liberals blamed Britain and the United States for the tension, a foretaste of their essential discomfort over America wielding power in the world or acting unilaterally even when America was the only country capable of wielding power and acting unilaterally against the totalitarian. Yet at least some Liberals were growing uneasy with Stalin's behavior in central Europe, and they were growing uncomfortable with past allies from the Popular Front.

Wallace, on the other hand, viewed with utmost alarm all of Washington's policies aimed at containing Communism. He feared that they would needlessly provoke Stalin, whom he yearned to see as the benign Uncle Joe of the war years. Wallace's supporters and a dwindling band of Liberals were apprehensive about offending the Russians and taking their eyes off the fascist threat. Here we see a habit of mind that has become an enduring theme of Liberal thought up to the present, to wit: anxiety over American leadership—"cowboy diplomacy" as it is called—as opposed to a more "mature" accommodation to "world opinion." The most recent beneficiary of world opinion's magisterial process was Colonel Moammar Gadhafi reigning from his fortified tent, untroubled and costing tens of thousands of his countrymen's lives while President Barack Obama and Secretary of State Hillary Clinton waited for world opinion to take shape.

By the second half of 1947, Wallace was mulling over a third-party presidential run, confident of the support of twelve million voters. He surmised this figure from the exultant crowds that turned out to hear him utter such sonorous stuff as "My field is the world." He strode a grand stage where, said he, "If I have importance, it is because of the ideas that I have come to represent. They are major ideas, indestructible and on the march." He spoke of "jobs, peace, and freedom" that "can be attained together and can make possible One World, prosperous and free, within our lifetime."[4] Wallace spoke often of One World attainable through the United Nations—none of Washington's unilateral stuff for this forward-looker. By the middle of 1947, Wallace was, observed William Harlan Hale, "seeing more and more of fewer and fewer people."[5] The people he saw were Popular Fronters, radical independents interested in a Third Party, and fellow traveling Communists embracing a radical view of American politics.

Wallace's supporters and the dwindling band of Liberals still with him perceived two great menaces in the immediate postwar period: the resurgence of fascism and the presence of monopoly capitalism. Drawing their conclusions from a static view of economics, these alarmists on the left feared an economic phantasm very troubling to them in those days; though today, if mentioned at all, it is only in the mutterings found in the dank corners of the *Nation* magazine or on the wilder frontiers of the lunatic fringe. The condition is "scarcity economics."

Pursuing scarcity economics, the giant monopolies make their products scarce and charge gigantic markups for them. The lowly consumer has no substitutes available, and no producer comes in to offer one. This is what happens when the giant monopolies are in cahoots with the government. It is not what happens with free markets, which makes one at least wonder as to why leftists of a skeptical frame of mind did not at least contemplate free markets after World War II. For that matter, why have today's Liberals, witnessing President Barack Obama's continued bailouts of, for instance, Wall Street, AIG, Chrysler, and General Motors, not been reminded of their ancestors' old bugbear, scarcity economics? Possibly crony capitalism is not so offensive to the left so long as it is governed by *their* cronies.

As 1947 came to an end, Wallace declared his third-party run on the Progressive ticket, though he eventually received a depressing 1,157,328 votes (2.37 percent of the vote). He finished in fourth place, behind Strom Thurmond's State's Rights Party. By now, however, Liberalism had toughened up. It beheld too many unsavory types around Wallace. Walter Reuther, head of the United Auto Workers, took the measure of the Wallace movement when he said: "I think Henry is a lost soul . . . Communists perform the most complete valet service in the world. They write your speeches, they do your thinking for you, they provide you with applause and they inflate your ego." Alex Rose of the Liberal Party saw Wallace as doing Moscow's work in opposing the Marshall Plan. As Rose saw it, Wallace "accepted the viewpoints of Vishinsky and Molotov that our government is war-minded and Wall Street–dominated."[6] It did not take Joseph McCarthy or Richard Nixon to start the "Red Scare" of the late 1940s. In those days there really were Reds, and an increasing number of Liberals identified them eloquently.

At the end of February 1948, the Communists staged a coup d'état in Czechoslovakia, sometimes referred to as the Third Defenestration of Prague, that left the democratically

elected Czech leader Jan Masaryk dead on the pavement below his office in the Ministry of Foreign Affairs. The tough-minded Liberals joined most Americans in denouncing the Communist coup, and Wallace's campaign was left reeling. At first he blamed the Truman Doctrine, calling the Soviet's "get tough" policy a natural reaction to our "get tough" policy. Then, at a press conference, he spoke of the Communist coup as an understandable response to a right-wing plot in Prague, which he claimed was abetted by the American ambassador there. He offered no evidence. Another theory he came up with was that Masaryk suffered from depression over a recent cancer or brought on by the dreadful shape the world was in. Wallace was becoming desperate. A few months later, when the Soviets blockaded Berlin, Wallace wanted to withdraw from the beleaguered city.

Imagine: America came that close to having a card-carrying zany in Lincoln's bed. Had President Roosevelt died six months earlier, Vice President Wallace would have been our Commander-in-Chief.

The Prague coup was the beginning of the end for Wallace. The tough-minded Liberals were multiplying. Through books, essays, journalism, and the ADA, they distinguished themselves from the soft left around Wallace, and they eventually supported Truman's candidacy. He was not so bad after all. He had moved somewhat left.

They moved somewhat right. They all opposed Wallace and his self-proclaimed Gideon's Army.

A generation earlier, in the era of the Wisconsin progressive Robert La Follette the elder, the distinction between a Liberal and a Communist was one that the good Liberal was careful to maintain, but in the 1930s and prior to the Liberals' First Civil War, the good Liberals' vigilance against Communism faltered out of overarching concern for events taking place in Germany, Italy, Spain, and even in America where Liberals perceived fascist stirrings: the Coughlinites, the Townsendites, and the Rev. Gerald L. K. Smith.

Then along came World War II, and the Soviets were our allies. President Roosevelt had his hands full with Nazi and Japanese espionage and was naturally chary about prosecuting Communist spies, too, though the FBI and other government investigators were closing in on some. The Hatch Act investigations of 1942 revealed evidence that both Alger Hiss and Harry Dexter White were in fact Communists, but they denied it, and anyway the war effort commanded Washington's full attention.

After the war, when domestic Communism became a matter of partisan politics, the Democrats closed ranks to protect themselves from charges that they were "soft on Communism." Hiss became a cultural hero with some American Liberals, though the Venona project, begun in 1943 to keep tabs on Stalin's intentions vis-à-vis staying in

the war, had gathered plenty of evidence that Hiss and 348 other Americans had been in contact with their Soviet handlers. The Hiss episode became the first Big Lie of postwar American politics, tremendously embittering both the left and the right.*

In 1948 people like Reuther and Rose, and a rising light, the scholar-activist Arthur M. Schlesinger Jr., labored sedulously to establish the distinction once again between Liberal and Communist or fellow traveler. The result was what Schlesinger called the Liberalism of "the Vital Center," a politics that spurned both fascism and Communism, locating Liberalism at the very center of American life. Schlesinger and like-minded Liberals insisted that Liberalism was mainstream American politics. The fashionable talk about the alienation of the intellectual and the angst of it all that was to overwhelm various precincts of the left in the 1960s was not for him. His Liberals were as American as apple pie, and it was the Republicans along with fascists and Communists who were out of step with history.

---

* The Big Lies have continued, the most recent being "Bush lied and people died," referring to President George W. Bush's supposed reliance on lies to enter into war in Iraq. The *Kultursmog* banished all other explanations for war with Iraq by the autumn of 2003, though at the war's beginning most foreign intelligence agencies working for the major powers believed Saddam Hussein had weapons of mass destruction, and even his generals were duped. Actually, our invading army found in the Kurdish town of Khurmal clear signs of the recent presence of weapons of mass destruction, namely traces of the deadly toxins cyanide, ricin, and potassium chloride.

Thus began, in the late 1940s, the tendency of Democrats to call Republicans fascists when the temperature of partisanship turned up. It is an indication of the power of the *Kultursmog* that no Republican with an eye to survival would ever call a Democrat a Communist, despite what we have seen in the Liberals' dalliance with the Popular Front. That would be playing what the Democrats in the Clinton years began to call "the politics of personal destruction."[7]

Historian Alonzo Hamby exquisitely described the new breed of tough-minded Liberal in *Beyond the New Deal: Harry S. Truman and American Liberalism*. The Vital Center was characterized by "a slight tendency toward moderation, a decline of utopian hopes and aspirations, a somewhat stronger suspicion of powerful government, increasing doubts about the goodness of human nature."[8] In the past, Liberals had been enraptured by left-wing revolutions: the French Revolution, the Russian Revolution, and closer to their day, the Spanish Civil War. They had been sentimental believers in progress, but writers like the theologian Reinhold Niebuhr, who deeply influenced Schlesinger, had assayed all the bloodshed and duplicity of the wars of revolution, and he did not see history marching along a path of unbroken progress. In 1949 four books, according to Hamby, summed up the tough-minded Liberals' views: *Target: You* by Leland Stowe, *The Power of Freedom* by Max Ascoli, *Strategy for Liberals* by Irwin Ross, and, finally, *The Vital Center* by Schlesinger.

Stowe argued that the American middle class was targeted by fascist and Communist totalitarians and by monopolistic Big Business. He put his faith in the American middle class, which had defeated fascism and would defeat Communism, while providing economic security and civil liberties under the rule of law. Ascoli, citing Edmund Burke, Alexander Hamilton, and Alexis de Tocqueville, stressed the limitations of human nature. He carefully defined freedom, claiming human rights varied from culture to culture. There were no natural rights. With a swipe at Wallace's One World, he claimed no "super-state" would ever legislate or define freedom for all mankind.

Ross was perhaps the most pessimistic of the tough-minded Liberals and the most muddleheaded. He argued that a second Depression was inevitable, but eventually America would have a mixed economy to be mastered by a strong Progressive movement. Avoiding Communism, fascism, and even socialism, the federal government somehow would come to own the vast majority of big businesses. Then the best minds would direct an economy that, Ross insisted, would remain a free economy. Somehow Ross's polity would escape being called socialist because he said it would. Here we see the Progressives once again taking refuge in argument by assertion.

Ascoli was perhaps the most interesting of these thinkers. In the *Reporter* magazine, an intellectual review that he founded, he argued for "Liberalism without tears." Was he anticipating that goofball turn Liberalism took three decades later when most of its leading candidates, certainly for presidency and probably for lower office, all affected "Liberalism awash in tears," occasionally "Liberalism awash in tears, sobs, and touching stories"? Running for the Democratic nomination became a very maudlin affair.

There were the Clintons blubbering about the youthful hell on earth they had somehow survived: he was a fat boy and so poor he ate bugs; she was called "Sister Frigidaire" even by her chums. Another tearjerker was Al Gore, wailing about the sufferings of his family, who raised him in squalor at Washington's posh Fairfax Hotel and sent him to the fashionable St. Albans whether he liked it or not, then to Harvard. In the summer they exposed him to the poison ivy and chiggers of a country estate in Tennessee. Then there were his nightmares about the whole planet's being on the brink. Actually there was a whole generation of crybabies in the Democratic Party resorting to this relatively unusual electoral ploy. The tears were pure theater, but they got the pols nominated at a national convention before a vast throng of sobbing, heaving delegates and not a few gullible media personalities who themselves probably imagined a Dickensian childhood and lives of unspeakable suffering.

Ascoli anticipated another Liberal weakness in 1949, arguing that "liberal values need to be thoroughly cleansed of triteness and smugness."[9] Of course, they were not, and today the triteness and smugness have become terminal. Had Ascoli and the *Reporter* lived on into the 1970s, it is a good bet that they would have become Neoconservatives. Some of the *Reporter's* writers did make the transition.

If Ascoli was the most interesting of the tough-minded Liberals, Schlesinger was the most energetic and interesting in his own right. He outlined a position in the late 1940s not all that different from the Neoconservatives of the 1970s. In fact, many Neocons in the 1970s could trace their politics from the Vital Center, though others were famously former Trotskyites. Schlesinger himself stayed with Liberalism until his death in February 2007, fattened up and domesticated by the New Frontier, the Great Society, and all the fun of the Clinton years. Still, in the first days of the Vital Center, he was a Liberal whom one could admire for his intelligence, eloquence, and collaboration with the likes of Niebuhr at the Vital Center.

Schlesinger cited both fascism and Communism as bringing down all the power of the state against human freedom, a point that previous Liberals seemed to have been mostly oblivious to. Certainly many seemed oblivious in the case of Communism. Schlesinger argued that both were the enemies of Liberalism. Fascism *and* Communism were hostile to the democratic center. Previously Liberals had held an optimistic view of man's nature, with mankind proceeding ever forward in what Wallace had beheld as the March of Progress. They believed in human perfectibility. Schlesinger denied it, and the recent World War seemed to prove him right. Moreover the idealism claimed by Communists and the romance of the Russian revolution were a cloud behind which terrible acts against humanity had been committed.

According to Schlesinger, Liberalism should have no illusions and should break with the Popular Front and Communism lest Liberalism destroy itself. Schlesinger called for a new Liberalism—or as he described it, a new "radicalism."[10] The new radicalism would maintain "a belief in the integrity of the individual, in the limited state, in due process of law, in empiricism and gradualism."[11] It was suspicious of concentrations of power and called for the mixed economy, featuring partial government control of the economy, planning, antitrust, and a welfare net to protect the most vulnerable citizens.

In foreign policy, Communism was to be contained and democracy encouraged through economic reconstruction. Schlesinger favored Containment, the Truman Doctrine, and the Marshall Plan. He denied that they were provocative but, rather, maintained they were prudent safeguards for democracy. He would, after due deliberation, use the threat of force to enforce these policies.[12] Force, then, had a place in Schlesinger's foreign policy, though as the years passed and the threats to American national security became more complex, Schlesinger became increasingly reluctant to use force, eventually coining the phrase "the Imperial Presidency."

The organization that was set up in early 1947 to champion the new Liberalism was the Americans for Democratic Action (ADA), and it derived great legitimacy from the number of New Dealers joining its ranks, among them Eleanor Roosevelt and Franklin Roosevelt Jr., then a politician full of promise. Another prominent politician in the ADA was the mayor of Minneapolis Hubert Humphrey, who would be a tough-minded Liberal force for years to come.

The ADA could take satisfaction in seeing its enemy, the Progressive Party, routed in 1948. Yet the ADA had significant weaknesses. For one, it was schizophrenic about the Democratic Party. Some members were scorned as "professional politicians" for wanting to embrace the party. Others, being more idealistic and philosophical, wanted to stay clear of partisan politics.

Also, what was the ADA to do about the South? There were Liberal impulses beating down there, but segregation and discrimination played an overwhelming role in the South of the 1940s. Schlesinger suggested addressing the economic problems of Dixie while leaving the question of civil rights subordinate for the time being—an evasion that brief decades later would be considered a shocking lapse into racism. The whole matter was hopeless, with even many

Southern Liberals being unsound on racial issues. Moreover, elsewhere in the country, civil rights was fast becoming one of Liberalism's foremost issues. ADA's Southern strategy was futile.

Then, too, the Democratic Party of the 1940s was very different from the party it is today. The ADA had to contend with diverse centers of power, Southern conservatives, urban machines, Western Progressives, anticommunist labor unions (a significant source of financial support, though many ADA members wanted to limit labor's contributions), and ethnic groups with roots often behind the Iron Curtain. Unlike the Democratic politics of the 1960s, there were few militant blacks or feminists, to say nothing of gays, transsexuals, or any of the other bizarre political identities that have contributed to what the contemporary Liberal historian Sean Wilentz has called the Democratic Party's fragmentation. Wilentz has identified another sign of Liberalism's death.[*]

Yet the ADA won the civil war of the 1940s and vanquished Wallace and his Gideon's Army. As the ADA looked to the 1950s, however, two themes were troubling. They

---

[*] "Plagued by divisions of race, ideology, and political temperament that dated back to the late 1960s; unable to unite around a coherent set of attitudes, let alone ideas about foreign policy and the military or domestic issues; beholden to a disparate collection of special constituencies and interest groups, each with its own agenda," Wilentz finds the Democratic Party "quarrelsome." Sean Wilentz, *The Age of Reagan: A History, 1974–2008* (New York: Harper, 2008), 268.

talked of using force to strengthen their foreign policy, but they really did not like the American military. Also they did not very much like business, especially laissez-faire economics and the economics of the Giant Corporations. The themes endure right up to the present. Before using America's military, Liberals await world opinion's approval, and they usually prefer vulnerable opponents. In the treatment of business, Liberalism has become antibusiness, which it entoils in regulations such as affirmative action, product safety, and energy regulations. Whether Big Business or small business, contemporary Liberalism wants to regulate it—killing commerce, killing personal freedom, and, of course, killing Liberalism.

4

LIBERALISM'S SECOND CIVIL WAR, 1968–1972 AND BEYOND

I t is fair to say that the presidency of Franklin Delano
Roosevelt represented a seminal moment in our history.
Before him there were things a president could not and
would not do. After him it was debatable, and the president
usually won the debate. In foreign and domestic policy, it
seemed the president could do almost anything as long as he
paused to offer a rationale abundant with high-toned ideals.
In the Schechter poultry case, FDR tried to regulate chicken
pluckers, but, as always, for lofty ideals. When he failed, he
threatened to pack the Supreme Court.

Certainly, this was true in Roosevelt's foreign policy.
FDR took us into World War II, despite neutrality laws and
despite the resistance of a sizable number of his countrymen. All to the good, most Americans have come to believe,
but at the time a certain vociferous minority, namely the iso-
lationists, had they access to today's Liberal values, would
have impeached FDR in the early 1940s for his foreign

policy intrigues. Hitler, Mussolini, and the Japanese milita-
rists would have been saved.

Before Roosevelt our foreign policy could be described
as nationalistic, though we confined our nationalism to the
Western Hemisphere. Roosevelt, employing charm and
cunning, extended it to the international stage. With such
rhetorical props as the Four Freedoms and later the veil of
what would become the United Nations, he set us up to
be Doctor of Democracy to the world. So it has been for
decades, until President Barack Obama came along to chide
America with such lines as "America has shown arrogance
and been dismissive, even derisive."[1]

At home Roosevelt imposed a package of social reforms
that changed American polity too. Before him America
had been entrepreneurial and individualistic. Roosevelt
revived the Progressives' antibusiness bias after the 1920s
Republicans' pro-business interregnum. Now, with his New
Deal, entrepreneurism and individualism were vaguely
suspect.

President Harry S. Truman secured the Roosevelt revolution in foreign and domestic policy. Thenceforth every
American president shared the idealism in foreign affairs
with varying passion until Obama came along. Dwight
Eisenhower was the least passionate; his successor, John F.
Kennedy, perhaps the most passionate. Kennedy was, however, murdered and became something rare in politics, a

true icon—not a mere celebrity or, as President Bill Clinton's episodic apologists gush of him, a "rock star"—but a venerated icon.

As historian David Reynolds has observed in his challenging *America, Empire of Liberty*, Kennedy in death became epochal. He was made,

> like Lincoln in 1865, into a martyr. JFK, of course, has always seemed youthful and glamorous—in marked contrast with Lincoln's gauche public manner—yet his domestic record to date had been unimpressive and in foreign affairs . . . early disasters had only just been redeemed by his handling of the Cuban missile crisis. But assassination simplified everything, making Kennedy, like Lincoln, a symbol of his age."[2]

Perhaps, had he lived, he would have given Liberalism the lift it needed, though I doubt it. Yet, almost for a certitude, he would not have hastened its demise as did his successor, Lyndon B. Johnson.

All the tendencies for overreach, overspending, bureaucratic clumsiness, and unaccountability that are endemic to the Liberal project flourished in LBJ's Great Society, an orgy of government excess far beyond the most lavish excesses of the New Deal. Though few commentators have recognized it, it was left to Richard M. Nixon to sort out all the problems Johnson had created, and Nixon tried to synthesize the Liberalism of the Great Society with the rising conservatism of the country. It was hopeless.

Nixon did welcome both the members of the conservative movement and their new converts, the Neocons, into his White House. He succeeded in cleaning up LBJ's messes in foreign policy, particularly with Beijing and Moscow, but Nixon was removed from office before he could focus on the domestic side. Otherwise, Nixon played a very important role for Liberals. He gave them something crucial to their peculiar politics, a satanic figure. Liberals have difficulty conceiving of evil in conventional terms. The disgraced Nixon served them well.

It fell to President Gerald R. Ford to deal with Nixon's ghost. President Jimmy Carter returned America to Liberalism and revealed its advanced state of enfeeblement in domestic and foreign policy: stagflation at home and humiliation abroad. He was badly beaten at the polls by the next seminal figure in American history, Ronald Reagan. In both foreign and domestic policy, President Reagan changed America, possibly forever. Even Obama shied away from running on a platform of raising taxes and spending madly, though on that last count he soon outdid himself, bringing the country to the brink of bankruptcy. We have yet to see if Obama's policy of bringing America into conformity with the "world conscience" and the "community of nations" replaces Roosevelt's realpolitik on behalf of American idealism. I have the gravest doubts. Liberalism, R.I.P.

Through the years, American Liberalism changed from the soaring eagle that Roosevelt had created, and all subsequent presidents at least tolerated, to an entirely different creature. Think of it as an ostrich. It is still a bird, but it hides from the outside world, from its fellow Americans, and, on the psychiatric level, from reality.

The New Politics, as it was called, emerged in the late 1960s, and it did not want to be part of the Vital Center of American politics. Rather, it was alienated and existential and suffered all the other claptrap diagnoses of the time. It wanted to move the Center far to the left, well beyond what Arthur M. Schlesinger and his colleagues had formulated in the late 1940s. The New Politics was like earlier reform movements: affluent, moralistic, educated, know-it-all. Only it had a self-conscious youth movement, which intensified everything. Increasingly it became the domain of feminists, black militants, and all the other *enragés* festering on the outer frontiers of politics. It, by 1972, presented the Democratic Party with a second civil war, and this time radicalism won.

By then it was variously called the New Politics, "the movement," and ultimately "McGovern's Army." Its critique of America, or of "Amerika," as the comrades spelled it, was more detailed by 1972 than anything Henry Wallace had come up with twenty-four years earlier. Its antipathy to businessmen and to the military was exacerbated by years of learned treatises and shocking revelations. It really hated business, going well beyond the New Deal's suspicions of Big Business to an aversion to *all* business as greedy, materialistic, a threat to the environment, and to the basic humanity of the citizenry.

To a whole string of the New Politics' Good Causes, business posed a threat. Business had to be regulated and taxed and constantly subjected to the watchful eye of government. The New Politics took up with red-hot ardor Eisenhower's term, "the military-industrial complex," for even the non-movement Liberal found the employment of force disturbing. Moreover, the New Politics was intolerant of dissent. This was in keeping with its Marxist and Progressive origins.

One of America's finest historians of Liberalism, Alonzo Hamby, explained the New Politics in theory and in practice: "Advocates of the New Politics conceived of politics as a moral and intellectual exercise and were contemptuous of the jockeying for relatively marginal advantages that characterized the interplay of organized interest groups. They saw themselves as uniquely suited to be protectors of the poor and unorganized, arbiters of the national good, tribunes of peace and order in an irrational world."[3] Theodore White, writing in *The Making of the President—1972*, described the bearers of the New Politics as policy wonks in priestly robes: "However much the real world might fear the liberal programs, it [America] must submit because *programs were morality*, even after programs had gone wrong in visible practice."[4] White was writing in his usual gaseous fashion, but he was stunned by the radicalism and arrogance of the New Politics, as were other Liberal observers who were slowly showing signs of sobriety.

The New Politics standard-bearer in the upcoming election would be Senator George McGovern. McGovern first ran for the presidency in 1968 in a three-week campaign as a stand-in for the assassinated Robert Kennedy. Apparently no one thought anything of it, and the forces that beat Wallace in 1948—now the Liberal Establishment of 1968—nominated Vice President Hubert Humphrey as their candidate. With their combination of big-city machines, Big Labor, the stalwart South, the party's rank and file, and the remnants of the Vital Center, they were overwhelmingly powerful. Yet outside the Chicago Convention in 1968, there had been rioting in the streets, and even inside, the New Politics made a dreadful scene. So as a gesture to the New Politics, the Establishment promptly agreed to set up the Commission on Party Structure and Delegate Selection for the 1972 Convention to avoid a repeat of the problems of 1968.

Called the Reform Commission, it got its chairman on February 8, 1969, when the head of the Democratic National

Committee, Senator Fred Harris, a Liberal sympathetic to the New Politics, chose that man again, George McGovern. An intense 1960s Liberal and dove, Senator Harold Hughes, had sought the chairmanship of the Reform Commission as a step toward the presidential nomination, but Humphrey vetoed him for his refusal to support the Democratic ticket in 1968. McGovern promptly made Hughes vice chairman. The Establishment remained insensate.

With Hughes, Harris, McGovern, and other sympathizers to the New Politics dominating the Reform Commission, the Establishment should have recognized that something was afoot. Big Labor and other party leaders, however, remained aloof. Possibly they did not understand that the New Politics had its roots back in the Wallace movement that they had defeated in 1948. Some, after twenty years of Liberal blah, had come to share the New Politics' aversion to business and to the military. Others were complacent. All were more concerned with "danger on the right" than "the real danger on the left." They were not ready for a reprise of the 1948 civil war, and anyway there were no Communists around McGovern as there had been around Wallace. Finally, the Reform Commission would probably be like other committees in Washington. The staff would do the work. This staff, however, was led by the youthful Gary Hart, a practitioner of the New Politics who would move on to the McGovern campaign in June of 1970.

The Reform Commission instituted one reform for the 1972 convention that was to have colossal significance for the Democratic Party and eventually on the country as a whole: affirmative action. Blacks, women, and youth (persons under thirty and over eighteen) were to be represented in state delegations as they were represented in the state. With that reform, the 1972 convention was handed to the New Politics.

At some point in 1972, the McGovern campaign became McGovern's Army, vaguely reminiscent of Wallace's Gideon's Army of 1948. But there was a difference. State primaries had multiplied, and McGovern's Army could move through them like a guerrilla force. The guerrillas were as confrontational as Gideon's Army had been, but this time they were fighting within the Democratic Party. McGovern's Army could overcome the Establishment leadership in a state and move on with hardly anyone taking notice.

By the time McGovern got to the convention, it was all over for the Establishment. Affirmative action and quotas would spread through all of American society eventually, but for now it mucked up only the Democratic Party. The Democratic Establishment did not know what hit them. Looking back on the nomination process a year later, White suggests the Establishment's astonishment at McGovern's achievement: "No one considered McGovern a serious Presidential contender, but he was everyone's personal favorite.... Robert Kennedy had called him 'the most decent man in the Senate.'"[5] Obviously, the tough-minded Liberals of 1948 had softened up by 1972. The Establishment did not expect "the most decent man in the Senate" to lead an insurrection.

All those years sitting around the Kennedys' swimming pool, at times being playfully heaved in by a drunken Teddy, had had their effect on Schlesinger. He and his colleagues in the Vital Center had had it good even in the Great Society. Now they went along for the ride in 1972. For them the fantasy world of endless American power and wealth had taken hold. There never would be a third civil war in the Democratic Party. When Arthur Schlesinger died on February 28, 2007, he died at a table in a chic Manhattan restaurant, supposedly with a Jack Daniel's Black at hand. He was eighty-nine. The Americans for Democratic Action survives even into the present, but it is indistinguishable from the zany left.

It is an inescapable fact: in 1968 the Democrats nominated their last serious candidate for the presidency, Hubert Humphrey. Possibly, one can argue that Walter Mondale was a serious candidate in 1984, but by then the country had moved on to the Reagan era. The reason for this astounding decline in leadership is apparent. With the McGovern reforms, the door opened for that creature peculiar to modern political life, the chronic campaigner. He is usually a

Democrat; he is always campaigning. McGovern ran for the 1972 presidential nomination from the 1968 convention on with hardly a break, though few in the old guard took him seriously. Jimmy Carter ran the most grueling campaign to date. Bill Clinton in retirement is still campaigning. Obama began his campaign for the presidency the day he entered the Senate and began his reelection campaign for 2012 earlier than any predecessor. There is only one problem with the chronic campaigner. He is a lousy chief executive. He cannot sit still and govern.

Viewed in hindsight, the Liberals' civil war of 1968–1972 was a reenactment of the Liberals' civil war of 1948, though without the Communists who sealed Henry Wallace's fate. McGovern actually had been at the 1948 Progressive Party National Convention as a Wallace delegate.

The son of a coal miner who became a preacher, McGovern had studied at Northwestern University to be a man of God in his own right, before switching to American history, where he earned a PhD. He wrote his thesis on the savagery of the corporations a generation before, though he ignored the savagery of the unions. It fixed his mind against modern business. He had exchanged the ministry for the professoriate, but he kept the ministry's otherworldly fervor.

By 1972 he was the perfect receptacle of all the New Politics' bilge. McGovern had spoken at the Washington Moratorium in November of 1969, flanked by banners of the Viet Cong. He favored amnesty for draft evaders and war resisters. He was for abortion, busing, and the more extreme positions of black militants. He was for lesser penalties for marijuana. He would have been a perfect guest at Leonard Bernstein's famous party for the Black Panthers. There were three constituencies that had especial saliency at the 1972 convention: blacks, women of the fevered brow, and the left-wing youth movement. McGovern favored them all.

As for his specific policies, three stand out as beyond the wildest hallucinations of Henry Wallace:

(1) a government grant of $1,000 annually for every man, woman, and child, rich or poor;

(2) a 37 percent reduction in the Pentagon budget from $87.3 billion in fiscal 1972 to $54.8 billion in 1975, the savings going to social welfare programs; and

(3) a rise in taxes, most strikingly on inheritance—no one would be able to receive more than half a million dollars from one's family in a lifetime or at the time of one's death!

As for the McGovern Army's great galvanic issue of the day, the Vietnam War, McGovern was for surrendering immediately, and he was only asking that peace-loving Hanoi return our POWs. In response McGovern would "liquidate" the government set up in Saigon six years earlier by a Democratic president. Now, that surpasses anything Wallace ever dreamed of, even abandoning Berlin, even blaming the Third Defenestration of Prague on an American ambassador.

Equally radical was the rhetoric of this famously mild, endearingly humorous old shoe, "the most decent man in the Senate." "Our government," he said, "would rather burn down schoolhouses and schoolchildren in Asia than build schools for Americans at home." Of Nixon he said, "The Nixon bombing policy on Indochina is the most barbaric action that any country has committed since Hitler's effort to exterminate Jews in Germany in the 1930s," and "He's playing with the lives of American soldiers and with American prisoners rotting in their cells in Hanoi. He's putting his own political selfish interest ahead of the welfare of these young Americans."[6]

McGovern lost to Nixon by the second greatest landslide in American history. He did not even win his home state. Even the youth vote eluded him. Yet defeat at the polls did not trouble practitioners of the New Politics that much. They pursued their politics starting in the 1960s along a broad front in the courts, in the regulatory bodies, in the *Kultursmog.*

It began with McGeorge Bundy, once a Harvard dean and national security advisor to Presidents Kennedy and Johnson, taking over the Ford Foundation. He introduced a new kind of philanthropy called "advocacy philanthropy." It preferred activism to the usual research then done in Liberal think tanks to develop expertise in governance and public policy. "Soon," James Piereson has written, "Ford and other liberal [Liberal] donors were investing in a maze of activist groups promoting feminism, affirmative action, environmentalism, disarmament, and other cutting edge causes. The Environmental Defense Fund, the Natural Resources Defense Council, the Women's Law Fund, and the Mexican American Legal Defense and Education Fund were among the products of this initiative."[7] All these groups advocated ideas, policies, legislative initiatives, and government regulations that could be manipulated in the courts and outside the normal electoral process on behalf of their ardent enthusiasms.

So McGovern's defeat did not set back the Liberal project completely. Yet the newly radicalized Liberals had reason to worry. Had they studied the polls, they would have seen what Teddy White saw: suppressed turnout even in Democratic strongholds. Rank-and-file Democrats often did not share in the New Politics' enthusiasms for quotas, feminism, and black militancy. Ethnics had been excluded from the quotas. Abortion was offensive to many. The New Democratic Party had shunted them aside. White summed it up:

> Even more perplexing were the final November results in
> the big-city Congressional races. Wherever in previously

solid Democratic districts the most colorful messengers
of the new theology had captured upset nominations
from old regular Congressmen, the final Democratic
results in November all fell off. In Denver, Colorado,
the new Democratic peace nominee lost the previously
solid Democratic seat in the 1st Colorado Congressional.
In the 3rd Massachusetts Congressional, north of Boston
(a mixed district of Catholic working class, Jewish
middle class, student activists), Father Robert F. Drinan
led his Republican rival by only 5 points where in 1968
the incumbent Democrat had led the Republican by 19
points. In the 7th California District (Berkeley-Bay Area),
Ronald V. Dellums led the Republican by 14 points in
1970—as against 33 points for his predecessor in 1968.
In the 19th New York, Bella S. Abzug won by 9 points—
as against the 20-point margin by which her defeated
regular rival in the primaries, Congressman Leonard
Farbstein, had scored over a Republican in 1968. . . . The
new politics, apparently, could mobilize for caucuses and
primaries and win victories inside the party—but it lost
force, in the strangest of ways, wherever it penetrated the
heart of cities.[8]

From the 1972 convention on, the New Politics brand of
Liberalism came to dominate the Democratic Party. With it
came the arrogance, the moral superiority, the insularity of

those privileged to partake of the most advanced thoughts, thoughts that have continued to evolve all these years: black equality, then black affirmative action; women's equality, then women's privileges; gay rights, then gay marriage. George Meany, the head of the powerful AFL-CIO, was treated shabbily at the 1972 convention and decided to take Big Labor and sit out the election. Here was the beginning of what in 1980 became the Reagan Democrats. Meany and Big Labor wanted tangible things, like jobs and the right to collective bargaining. Increasingly the Liberals, born of 1972, addressed *feelings*: feelings of empowerment, of entitlement, of *rage*. Ever since, a corruption has set in and led to even greater arrogance, insularity, and remoteness from the American mainstream.

From 1972 to the present, there has been an ongoing effort to appropriate federal money for identity politics, for the environment, for clean energy, for an ever-accumulating mass of Good Causes—always with little accountability. Thus today Obama would give federal money to Green Corporations. They supply jobs to newly configured unions that are mere make-work jobs. The tough union bosses of Meany's day are pretty much gone, replaced by frauds angling for jobs that are subsidized by the federal government. George Meany knew how an economy ran. Obama does not.

Sean Wilentz, the Liberal historian, saw it all coming when he wrote, "Plagued by divisions of race, ideology, and political temperament that dated back to the late 1960s; unable to unite around a coherent set of attitudes, let alone ideas about foreign policy and the military or domestic issues; beholden to a disparate collection of special constituencies and interest groups, each with its own agenda, the quarrelsome Democrats made the fractured Republican Party look like a juggernaut."[9] He wrote that in 2008, two years before the undertakers arrived to take charge of the Liberal corpse.

LIBERALISM

CAPRICCIO C

Left-wing historian Michael Kazin, in a grim but erudite *New York Times* essay, asked recently: "Whatever Happened to the American Left?" He proceeded bravely, "Sometimes, attention should be paid to the absence of news." He delved deeper: "How do you account for the relative silence of the left? . . . They [the left] fashioned their own institutions—unions, women's groups, community and immigrant centers and a witty, anti-authoritarian press—in which they spoke up for themselves and for the interests of wage-earning Americans." Alas: "Today, such institutions are either absent or reeling."[1] Another way of putting it is: Liberalism is dead.

In truth, it is amazing that Liberalism got this far given its intellectual origins. Looking back through the haze of history, one finds two rather implausible Founding Fathers for Liberalism or Progressivism, as the squeamish have called it. They are Jean-Jacques Rousseau of Geneva in the eighteenth century and Karl Marx of Trier, Prussia, in the nineteenth century. The first was a precursor to the limousine Liberals of modern times. He lived the good life. The second was a middle-class radical, a rabble-rouser of furious temperament, but a brilliant theoretician of kleptocracy. Both were extremely disagreeable and wondrously incompetent. You would never trust them to boil an egg, much less to throw eggs, or for that matter, Molotov cocktails. It is hard to imagine them as the founders of a movement, either a reformist movement like Liberalism, or the more virulent—and utterly unscientific, Marx notwithstanding— movement of world revolution known as Communism; but there you have it. I suspect that both would have been forgotten in history's wake if it were not for the rise, 250 or so years ago, of what Paul Johnson has called the "secular intellectual."

Nowadays, of course, the term *intellectual* has attached to it too many conflicting nuances to convey a settled meaning. For some people an intellectual is a good thing. For others it is a bad thing, even a ridiculous thing. I choose to call Johnson's secular intellectual a "Sage *manqué*," for despite his enormous intellectual ambitions, the Sage *manqué* was a failure. To be sure he was, as Johnson says, a new phenomenon in history and a contributing factor to the modern world. However, his various blueprints for the perfect society all failed. He did take the place of priests, scribes, or oracles—what was once called the *clerisy*. In fact, he replaced them all and went a step further. Untroubled by religious codes, traditions, collective wisdom, or the law, he formulated a new society shaped by his own godlike intellect. In the case of Rousseau and Marx, the Sage *manqué* left the water running, the front door open, and he forgot to empty the bedpan. Yet both Rousseau and Marx presumed to remake the world. Some called the Sage *manqué* a *philosophe*; others, an intellectual. I think by now, as we look back on the shambles they created, we can call most of the Sages *manqués* dreadful pests. As for Rousseau and Marx, they were also slightly deranged.

Liberals in their last years were very coy about Marx's intellectual bequest, for his contributions to at least the rhetoric of Lenin, Stalin, and Mao Zedong were bloody, brutal, and illiberal, however one chooses to define the term. He was, however, helpful to the Liberals as they developed their morose views of private property and the enormous disruptiveness of free commerce. Indeed, he was, as I have said, the world's chief theoretician of kleptocracy, which sees the state as benignly and irresistibly engaged in thievery.

About Rousseau, the Liberals were more frank, especially Liberals with a sense of history and romance in their blood. Not nearly so much of mankind was slaughtered, tortured, and enslaved in his name, at least once the French Revolution was out of the way (the revolutionaries idolized his memory). Moreover his lifestyle and intellectual legacy were so posh and confusing he gave Liberals something to dream about and, among the professoriate, something to argue about. What did he mean by the General Will? Did the Social Contract include primates? How did he get into all those salons and rub elbows with the aristos?

Actually Rousseau was the first manipulator of what came to be called the *Kultursmog*; perhaps the earliest puff-puff of it. He was a splendid communicator, a stupendous writer, and he even possessed elegant penmanship. In his day (1712–1778) there were no mass media to pollute, but there were salons to attend, public readings to dazzle, proclamations to nail on the wall, tracts to write, and books—books for the disgruntled aristocrats and other prerevolutionary malcontents. If Rousseau were alive today, he would be a regular on National Public Radio, a contributor to the *New York Times*, a member of the Council on Foreign Relations; perhaps he would win a Nobel Prize.

Marx, on the other hand, associated with a rougher crowd. Always middle class (he knew no workers), he cultivated the revolutionaries of 1848 and thereafter. He carried a gun at times, almost got arrested for using it in his college days, and associated with killers and the occasional bomb-throwers. Were he alive in 1970, he would have ducked out of a Greenwich Village bomb emporium just in the nick of time. He always left the risky work for others. In 2011 he would be in comfortable retirement with Bill Ayers and Bernardine Dohrn, and he would probably have a friend in the White House. He would be honored but still angry. He was always angry.

Both men attracted a cult-like following through the years, and their unsystematic, if fetching, prose encouraged it. The idolaters asked, what did they mean? They were the subjects of scholarly disputes, even altercations. In the case of Marx, who was far more brutal, there was always violence. His Russian disciple, Leon Trotsky, suffered an ice axe to the skull from a secret agent for his caviling. Countless others died in Stalin's famous purges, and Mao had his entire populace enslaved until he, without notice, jerked it around to side with the "capitalist roader," Richard Nixon. The scholars who compiled *The Black Book of Communism* put Communism's toll at approximately 100 million souls by the time the whole bloody endeavor was all over.[2]

In establishing their cults, Rousseau and Marx rather resembled Mohandas Gandhi in the twentieth century or Barack Obama at least for a while in the twenty-first century. I suspect that, like Gandhi, they knew how to push the right buttons in their day to get attention: Rousseau in the salons and with his fluent if chaotic tracts, Marx in the coffeehouses frequented by zanies and thugs and with his equally chaotic tracts. Write an inscrutable tract or at least a wildly contradictory one and gain a following of bemused eggheads.

Neither man was able to earn a living through conventional means, and each became an incessant sponger. They knew whom to cadge off of. Marx had the wealthy Friedrich Engels as a mark and Uncle Lion Philips who founded what in time became the sprawling Philips Electric Company. Rousseau had his hooks into a string of women. Both Rousseau and Marx were famous ingrates.

Rousseau was a deadbeat well into his thirties before he hit his stride in the salons and the chateaux of the great and the good and the decidedly hypocritical. Without success he tried thirteen jobs and failed at all of them from a cashier to a civil servant, an engraver, a farmer, lackey, musician, music-copier, seminary student, tutor, and finally a private secretary. He got that cushy post in 1743 from the French Ambassador in Venice, the Count de Montaigu, but after eleven months he had to flee the authorities. Montaigu later attested to Rousseau's "vile disposition," "unspeakable insolence," "high opinion of himself," and, in sum and in fine, "insanity."[3] It is a judgment that was eventually arrived at by practically everyone who had ever befriended him and many who had not; an instance of the former is Diderot and of the latter is Voltaire.*

---

* Professor I. W. Allen summed up Rousseau's faults thus: he was a "masochist, exhibitionist, neurasthenic, hypochondriac, onanist, latent homosexual afflicted by the typical urge for repeated displacements, incapable of normal or parental affection, incipient paranoiac, narcissistic introvert rendered unsocial by his illness, filled with guilt feelings, pathologically timid, a kleptomaniac, infantilist, irritable and miserly." Paul Johnson, *Intellectuals* (New York: Harper & Row, 1988; Phoenix Press, 2000), 26. Citations refer to the Phoenix edition.

Montaigu thought him bound to live a life of poverty. Little did the Ambassador realize how crafty his former employee was to become at fleecing the saps.

Marx, too, never seriously considered work and spent much of his life broke and sponging. He received a considerable inheritance from his family and promptly blew it. After settling in London, having fled the continent, he subjected his beautiful wife and their children to improvidence and a Bohemian life until the mid-1840s when he began cadging off of Engels. His diatribes against usury, the capitalist system, and class owe much to his incompetence with money.

Karl Marx's entire theory of class is based on anti-Semitism. He seems to have found the bourgeoisie and Jews inseparable. Indeed he was a bitter anti-Semite despite his family being born Jewish—and despite being from a line of distinguished rabbis on both sides to boot. He was also a racist. He called his son-in-law, Paul Lafargue (a Cuban with some black blood), "Negrillo" or "the Gorilla." Both qualities were highlighted in his violent disputes with fellow members of the left. He called the labor organizer Ferdinand Lassalle "the Jewish Nigger" and "a greasy Jew disguised under brilliantine and cheap jewels," and he wrote to Engels on July 30, 1862, "It is now perfectly clear to me that, as the shape of his head and the growth of his hair indicates, he is descended from the

Negroes who joined Moses' flight from Egypt (unless his mother or grandmother on the father's side was crossed with a nigger). This union of Jew and German on a Negro base was bound to produce an extraordinary hybrid."[4]

Rousseau loved his cat. There is a scene, chronicled by James Boswell, of Rousseau playing with the cat quite joyfully. He also loved his dog, Sultan, and an earlier dog, Turc. Yet humanity always let him down. In his book *Émile* he dwelt on education, seeing it as a panacea for mankind, much as later Liberals did. However, there is no evidence that he ever observed children in any situation, much less in an educational setting. It was all idle speculation. He had five children with his mistress, an illiterate laundress, and sent them immediately to a hospital for abandoned waifs without seeing them or naming them. It is improbable that any survived.

Rousseau was rude, antisocial, megalomaniacal, quarrelsome, occasionally given to bizarre dress, and mentally ill. He seemed to suffer paranoia. The aristos and would-be revolutionaries loved it. For years he lived off of Madame Françoise-Louis de Warens, whose source of income was a royal pension. When she suffered through her last days, penniless and lonely, he ignored her. By then he was flying high, but he had acquired many enemies. Voltaire summed him up as "a monster of vanity and vileness."[5] As the cult grew up around his ghost, Sophie Countess d'Houdetot, reflecting back on him in 1813 from a great old age, recalled her famous lover: "He was ugly enough to frighten me and love did not make him more attractive. But he was a pathetic figure and I treated him with gentleness and kindness. He was an interesting madman."[6] The cult grew despite all his critics. One has to wonder, why? Is there something about the Liberal that invites gullibility?

Rousseau's books and letters are laced with half-truths and arrant lies. *Émile* and the *Confessions* stand out. J. H. Huizinga, a modern-day scholar, writes of the *Confessions* that "the more attentively one reads and re-reads, the deeper one delves into this work, the more layers of igno-miny become apparent."[7] Paul Johnson writes, "What makes Rousseau's dishonesty so dangerous—what made his inventions so rightly feared by his ex-friends—was the diabolical skill and brilliance with which they were pre-sented."[8] And Johnson quotes biographer Lester Crocker, "All his accounts of his quarrels (as in the Venetian epi-sode) have an irresistible persuasiveness, eloquence and air of sincerity; then the facts come as a shock."[9] Rousseau was one of the great mountebanks of history, but he was not without his gifts.

His political musings were more widely cast than those of Marx and thus inspired a wider audience of Liberals. Besides, his legacy was not so bloody. As for his critique of private property, it was slightly out of focus compared to Marx's, but it compelled a broad spectrum of modern Liberals: socialists, environmentalists, moralists, and some consumerists. He merely distrusted private property. He thought the competition for property led to all sorts of criminal behavior. Writing as the Industrial Revolution approached, with accumulations of wealth for more than two hundred years—wealth for rich and for the poor and those in between—Rousseau theorized an early critique of capitalism. Had he written as a Trappist monk with the point of view of a stoic, he might have had a point. But he was writing as a materialist, presumably as a man who would someday like to have owned a computer, a color television, a sports car, or at least bought a ticket for the subway. His critique made little economic sense.

In the preface to his play *Narcisse* and in his *Discours sur l´inégalité* he obsessed over property and the acquisition of it as the primary cause of a condition that was to transfix Marx and generations of leftists thereafter, *alienation*. Another idea he had was his blah about cultural, evolution. To Rousseau "natural" meant pre-cultural, which was good. As with children, so with aborigines and Red Indians; he never met one. Cultural meant mankind in association with one another. It meant society, and that meant trouble. As he wrote in *Émile*, "Man's breath is fatal to his fellow men."[10] Presumably he was an early environmentalist. Yet the culture in which men live can be manipulated, he thought, and should be manipulated by the best minds. Thus Rousseau was an early proponent of social engineering.

Though he is inconsistent and contradictory in matters of politics, when it comes to his views on the state, Rousseau is as clear as a truncheon across the skull. The state should order every aspect of human behavior. Now you see why Liberals liked him.

His ideal state is more than an authoritarian state. It is totalitarian. There would be none of those checks and balances or federalism or the rule of law for Jean-Jacques. There is merely the state; and it is based on the General Will, which all must obey. The General Will at first strikes modern man as a mysterious thing, but Rousseau and his disciples see it as an instrument for social engineering to inculcate virtue. The General Will "is always righteous."[11] Who will read its chicken entrails and tell us what it means? Well, the best minds, or as Herbert Croly called them some 150 years later, the keepers of "a constructive national democracy," in a word, Progressives.[12] Interestingly, Rousseau might have been a favorite, too, of Benito Mussolini in the early twentieth century, whose central fascist doctrine stated, "Everything within the State, nothing outside the State, nothing against the State."[13] *Il Duce* just chose the wrong side.

"Everything," Rousseau wrote, "is at root dependent on politics." He went on, "Vices belong less to man than to man badly governed."[14] Politics and the state that politics creates are the universal cures for our ills. How could Liberals resist this man? And the high priority he put on politics only encouraged their lust for politics. Both conservatives and Liberals have had a healthy hankering for politics, but the political libido of the conservative is measured and restrained for the most part. The political libido of the Liberal has been the libido of a nymphomaniac, at times of a child molester. It has known no bounds, which in part explains why Liberalism is dead. It attempts too much. Some things are best left to religion, to the family, to the individual, to social organizations, or to the private eleemosynary impulse. Rousseau left everything to the state, which thrilled Liberals.

As mentioned earlier, Marx became extremely controversial with Liberals, particularly by the time of the Liberals' First Civil War. A lot was going on in Europe and in Asia, thanks to Stalin and to Mao Zedong, that did not go down well with American Liberals. Moreover Marx's ideas did not hold up very well. There were his ideas on private property and that brilliant if fanciful idea about alienation, but otherwise he was not very thoughtful, scholarly, or—his great boast— scientific. Much of his thought was lifted from Rousseau, or it was simply café anti-Semitism. I am afraid despite all the glowering busts of him around the world—now mostly torn down—he was a misanthrope. Like his superior Rousseau, he acquired a lot of critics in his lifetime, who were obviously right in their estimate of him. As Michael Bakunin put it in his final judgment of Marx: "Marx does not believe in God but he believes much in himself and makes everyone serve himself. His heart is not full of love but of bitterness and he has very little sympathy for the human race."[15]

Marx was a good writer and very aphoristic. In modern times he might have made a fortune writing jingles for Madison Avenue, assuming he could have gotten rid of his sempiternal rage with Valium or some other modern pharmaceutical wonder. He also had a sense of what is funny, as did Hitler. This perhaps explains in part how he kept some of his sorely pressed associates around him and his wife. They liked a good laugh. He was savage and caustic, but it was funny—more evidence of how effective he would be on Madison Avenue. Yet he had terrible work habits. He would never write a proper book in part because he merely let out bursts of bile but also because his work habits were so poor. *Capital* he envisaged as a six-volume work. He was lucky to complete one, and that one reads like a collection of essays.

He had a bad diet. He drank too much, and it gave him liver problems. He smoked too much, and a Prussian secret service agent gave a description of his apartment that sheds light on his habits and even his sanity:

There is not one clean and solid piece of furniture. Everything is broken, tattered and torn, with half an inch of dust over everything and the greatest disorder everywhere. In the middle of the [living room] there is a large, old-fashioned table covered with oilcloth and on it lie manuscripts, books and newspapers, as well as the children's toys, rags and tatters of his wife's sewing basket. . . . When you enter Marx's room smoke and tobacco fumes make your eyes water.[16]

That was in 1850 when the family had a housekeeper to keep things tidy. She was practically a slave to Marx's family for almost forty years, and he secretly impregnated her the very year this report was being written.

Marx slept irregularly and at odd hours, snoozing late into the day then frequenting his night haunts to excogitate his revolution and drink strong ale. How he could have imagined he would have time to write *Capital* is incomprehensible. He brings to mind one of those forty-five-year-old graduate students at one of our Midwestern cow colleges who bores his drinking companions with the great book he will write once he gets his PhD. All his life, Marx was extremely dirty. This, along with his dreadful nutrition, led to outbreaks of boils all over his body. He had them on his bottom when he was writing *Capital*, which doubtless added to the tome's irritable tone and disorderly structure. This could also explain the book's rancor toward the happy bourgeoisie and the Jews. He also had boils on his penis. Urologically, he was at one with

Rousseau, who suffered a mysterious dysfunction that gave him the need to urinate with embarrassing urgency, often as he put it "on some noble white-stockinged leg."[17]

At his best Marx was a good journalist, but even here he was slipshod. He stole lines from Jean-Paul Marat: "The workers have no country" and "The proletarians have nothing to lose but their chains." He also stole from Heinrich Heine: "Religion is the opium of the people,"[18] and there were others. He was even more slipshod in writing longer works, most notably his books and the tracts. Critics have accused him of purposely misquoting, distorting, and out-and-out lying. Two Cambridge scholars in the 1880s had at his book *Capital*. They found that quotations were often "conveniently shortened by the omission of passages which would be likely to weigh against the conclusions which Marx was trying to establish."[19] Then again they found that he was guilty of "piecing together fictitious quotations out of isolated statements contained in different parts of a Report. These are then foisted upon the reader in inverted commas [quotation marks] with all the authority of direct quotations from the Blue Books themselves." The Cambridge scholars concluded that their evidence showed "an almost criminal recklessness in the use of authorities."[20]

Marx's "scientific explanation" of history was a mere collection of random daydreams, many decidedly disagreeable, for which he fabricated facts and data in support. Much of his other writing involved prophecies, all of which have been proven false by the abundance of free market economics and by democracy's protection of human rights. Today, when one reads of a Marxist regime, say Robert Mugabe's Marxist regime, one does not think of exulted reading rooms where learned-gogues, radiant with the Marxist gibberish, apply the Master's work to current problems. One thinks of row upon row of dreary barracks populated by moronic troops waiting to carry out their leader's whimsy.

Rousseau and Marx were once illustrious names in the political philosophy of the West. What was wrong with the West? Well, Rousseau and Marx and the other Sages *manqués* came at the end of an era and were more entertaining than the Bourbons, the Hohenzollerns, the Habsburgs, and Romanovs who were just hanging on. At least Rousseau and Marx wrote better. They also offered an alternative vision, not the best vision but a better vision than the *ancien régime*. Perhaps we should not be too hard on the profs and the other Liberals for their advocacy of these fantasists. I would not want to be governed by a Bourbon duke any more than by a Marxist commissar or by one of Rousseau's whiz kids. Thankfully, I do not have to be. Beginning in 1789, America had George Washington. Then there was Abraham Lincoln. Along the way came hundreds, perhaps thousands, of political leaders advised and counseled by the Constitution, and there was Franklin Roosevelt, who at least did save the world from Hitlerism, and then came Ronald Reagan, who saved us from Marx's progeny and revived the economy.

Beginning in 1787, we had the Founding Fathers to guide us. Their work has served us well, and their revival today comes in the nick of time. Is it not rather amazing that the Founding Fathers' work has guided this nation for more than two hundred years while the Sages *manqués* made a dreadful hash of things everywhere?

6

THE INFANTILE LEFT AND THE STEALTH SOCIALIST

P resident Franklin Delano Roosevelt, it is said, relished campaigning. It refreshed him. It gave him renewed strength. I cannot recall anyone, prior to Roosevelt, reveling in the ongoing scrum that is a presidential campaign, though his distant cousin, Theodore Roosevelt, probably loved it too. Teddy was the type (and, by the way, an early advocate of Progressive policies, from which, as we have seen, Liberalism sprang). By "campaigning" I mean the ephemeral aspects of it, not a presidential debate or a momentous speech, such as Bryan's Cross of Gold speech or Kennedy's speech on his Catholicism. I refer to the frenzy of the crowd, the kissing of babies, the eating of sometimes disgusting ethnic food—all occasions for the photo-op.

However, from those delirious events that FDR relished, campaigning has declined, at least for one class of politicians, into sophomoric exhibitionism; and for them it is sheerest fun. Its adepts usually are found among the Infantile Leftists. On the campaign trail they throw Frisbees, make funny faces, jog and skip, anything for a photo-op. Some even imagine the presidency to be fun, and for President Bill Clinton it mainly was, despite some close calls along the way to the White House and closer calls once there. The Clintons come from this class of politicos, he talking about his underwear to teenagers and playing a saxophone, she downing shots in the Indiana primary; the Gores engaging in the longest, most impassioned kiss ever recorded at a national political convention; and Jean-François Kerry, windsurfing, duck hunting (twelve days before the presidential election!), perhaps bungee jumping, possibly skateboarding with a baseball cap on backwards, or how about a beret?—his antics are particularly sophomoric.

Then there is Barack Obama. He is a different type of politico altogether, as we shall see. It is hard to picture him having the sheerest fun ever. He is *the* Stealth Socialist. From the start he was odd even by these campaign standards. Possibly that comes with being a community organizer, from which he briefly became a U.S. senator, then president of the United States, probably for one term. For decades he sat through long, hysterical tirades from the Reverend Jeremiah Wright. He associated with grim company: for instance, Bill Ayers and Bernardine Dohrn. As president he has been indecisive but somehow ideologically rigid. He is different.

At any rate, something has been changing in the Democratic Party from the New Deal to the New Frontier to the Great Society and on. Walter Mondale in 1984 was possibly the last of the classic Democratic candidates, courting labor, courting ethnics, playing to the urban machines. Yet, he was also transitional, roaming the country, intoning melodramatically, "Where's the heart? Where's the soul?" Discoursing on one's underwear, downing shots, French-kissing one's wife on national television, windsurfing, and all the other hijinks of recent years do not bespeak the qualities of a great statesman, but they do bespeak a show-boating pol having a colossal good time. Liberalism may be dead, but its zombies have not stopped seeking high office. Their antics get ever more amusing . . . and narcissistic.

Fittingly, I suppose, politics-as-hijinks began when that youthful aide to George McGovern during Liberalism's Second Civil War, Gary Hart, sought the presidency in 1984. Hoping to run against President Ronald Reagan—who, incidentally, most certainly would have slaughtered him—the first Infantile Leftist, the Honorable Hart, claimed an especial affinity to the mystery of High Technology, to the rumble bumble of The Future, and in the fullness of time, to the arrantly weird. In this he was competing with another early Infantile Leftist, the weirdo Jerry Brown, who added food fads and yoga to his list of bizarre priorities. By the way, Hart called himself—at least transiently—a

Neoliberal following Irving Kristol's Neoconservatives, but the Neocons were Liberals who had sobered up and made the transition to conservatism. All Hart ever was was a Liberal who had adopted a trendy prefix before becoming a Liberal again.

Hart's campaign foundered in 1984 over gaffes on the campaign trail and revelations that he had surreptitiously changed his name in 1961 from Gary Hartpence to Gary Hart. There were also discrepancies over his age, repeated cosmetic surgery to his signature, and two unexplained separations from his wife. When he ran again in 1988, he utterly blew up when it was found that he regularly broke from the campaign trail to canoodle at least one "model," Donna Rice, ultimately on the yacht—I do not make these things up—the *Monkey Business*.[1] He was photographed with the cutie on his lap and an official *Monkey Business* tee shirt on his person.

What serious candidate for high office dissembles about his age, his signature, and his name? And the cutie? How could he imagine that all this would not be discovered? He actually challenged the press to follow him! Hart or Hartpence or perhaps just Pence was the first of a string of national figures never before seen on the national stage, the weirdo, the living fiction, the contrived persona. The contrived persona is a figure that the ordinary American would not want to have living in the neighborhood, but that a goodly number of Americans would vote for this sociopath is manifest. It is another case of the electorate confusing *notoriety* for *distinction* and voting the notorious little creep into office. Hart never won the presidency, though he did test the waters again in 2002 and 2003. Still, he was a prototype: the weirdo sociopath who, running as a Democrat, sought the presidency.

Possibly at work here was some variation of the Chappaquiddick Dispensation. At any rate, in the years following Hart's presidential campaigns came more weirdos: Brown, the Clintons, Gore, Kerry, Edwards, and a dozen or so less famous (Governor Bill Richardson of New Mexico comes to mind)—all capering and mugging along the campaign trail. On the Republican side there were weirdos, too: Newt Gingrich, Terry Sanford, and probably a few more. Fortunately, the Republicans do not get very far. In the *Kultursmog* the double standard holds Republicans accountable. It is about the only salutary contribution made by the *smog*.

This motley band (I include Gingrich because he embraces almost all their characteristics, save he is a Republican) began its life in politics early. In college they can be spotted by historians as playing energetic roles in what earlier generations of students considered a mere student activity, student government. This was the 1960s, actually the second half of the 1960s, and the well-intentioned Liberals who ran American universities caved in to the demands of a new kind of student. America was rich, and suddenly students, too, were affluent. They had disposable income and time on their hands. Most got good grades, but none was particularly scholarly. They presumed that student government types should share in the governance of universities, and rather amazingly, Liberal profs and administrators did too. After all, these kids were also Liberals, at the time even Gingrich. The universities have never recovered.

The result was that student government became a haven for self-promoters, hustlers, narcissists, and other improbabilities. Most were hypocrites from the start, but all became hypocrites eventually. While other students were going about the pleasant pastime of being students, these "politicians" applied themselves to the drudgery of promoting themselves with the increasingly exhausted university administrations. We, in the 1960s, called them Coat-and-Tie Radicals, for they shared some of the radicalism of the fringe left while wanting all the usufructs and privileges of the upper bourgeoisie.

After college and grad school—possibly several grad schools—and probably the Peace Corps or life with a smelly Indian guru, they settled into one of the *Kultursmog-*approved professions. Then the unanticipated happened. Ronald Reagan was elected president, and for twelve years the Coat-and-Tie Radicals did not matter. America prospered. In the *smog* their legends proliferated: the 1960s generation was all left-wing and abounding with idealism, and Reagan was "sleepwalking through history," as a book about the Reagan years was titled. There was something about plastics and Mrs. Robinson, or was that earlier? It all eventually ran together, an endless chorus of sarcasm with no serious point.

Liberalism began to die. Then, *hesto presto*, something unforeseen happened. Ross Perot ran for the presidency in 1992 on a third-party ticket. His campaign was one of history's banana peels upon which the conventional wisdom slips. What is more, George H. W. Bush, who appeared so formidable in the polls in 1991, ran a lackluster campaign against an oft-caught liar, an oft-caught womanizer, a draft dodger, a serial liar, and an erstwhile Coat-and-Tie Radical, Bill Clinton. Suddenly this kind of lefty had a new lease on life. But how long would it last? Actually, about two years, and then the Republicans gained control of *both* chambers of Congress. In time, Clinton left a legacy of welfare reform, free trade, and balanced budgets—all Republican policies—along with his pronunciamento, "The era of Big Government is over." Oh yes, and Clinton was also impeached—the first elected president to suffer such a setback—while his supporters, most notably feminists, dismissed his misbehavior as being "only sex." Rape? Groping? The pathetic lovesick intern depicted by his aides as a stalker? As I say, Liberalism is dead.

By the pivotal election of 2010, we saw that the years had taken their toll on the 1960s Coat-and-Tie Radicals and their fellow travelers. They were now grown up but had only their delusions to sustain them, mainly that they were forever young. Truly they were the *Infantile* Left. Still narcissists, hustlers, and self-promoters, they now were victims of their inflated and preposterous biographies. They assumed that they were the heirs and heiresses to the New Deal, the New Frontier, to progress itself. When they gained fleeting power in 2006, they spent madly and called it a new New Deal. They passed an enormous amount of regulation and set the stage for that greatest delusion of all, the Age of Obama.

In the end there was not much of substance to the Infantile Leftists. They were poseurs and has-beens. Though now on the far side of middle age, they claimed to have found deep significance in rock 'n' roll, and bear in mind, these were about the only politicians left who could lay claim to the New Deal and the original Progressivism. They were supposed to have grown up. Every one of the aforementioned Infantile Leftists claims metaphysical significances for rock music. In February 2009 the sixty-seventh secretary of state, Hillary Clinton, recalled that in her angst-ridden days at Wellesley College, she turned to the Beatles—not to philosophy or to God—for whatever was tormenting her. "As I went through my angst period and struggled with the challenges of living in the real world [Wellesley College?] the more existential message struck home," she told Fox News. Existential message? She was speaking of the Beatles, four singers in their twenties with a TV viewer's education. She was a sixty-one-year-old woman and secretary of state. Thomas Jefferson had been among her predecessors. John Lennon and Paul McCartney "were geniuses," she assures her interviewer. "Hey Jude," is her favorite Beatles song, and she praises its "Biblical tone and seriousness."[2] Actually, according to the most persuasive critics, the song is about masturbation.

Another source of inspiration for the Infantile Leftists has been Mohandas Gandhi. Practically every one of them honors him as the Great Soul, though he is often pictured walking through the Indian dust, clad in an old sheet, a stick in his outstretched hand. Senator Kerry asks the Egyptian crowds demonstrating against Hosni Mubarak to apply the principles of Gandhi to their movement and those of Martin Luther King Jr. Yet, of course, Gandhi was a crank *and* one of the greatest self-promoters ever known. In fact, after considering all the aforementioned collegiate self-promoters, it is Gandhi who embodies every one of their unseemly traits along with a few of his own.

He was sexually bizarre, politically incompetent, and a zealous faddist. He advised the Jews and the Czechs to adopt nonviolence toward Hitler, claiming that "a single Jew standing up and refusing to bow to Hitler's decrees" would "melt Hitler's heart." He was a racist, at least toward the blacks of South Africa, complaining about being jailed with them and making repeated claims about their laziness and nudity.[3] His food fads were noted sometimes favorably with forward lookers, as was his enthusiasm for enemas. His first question in the morning to the comely young women who chastely shared his bed was, "Have you had a good bowel movement this morning, sister?"*

Yet, as I have mentioned, he was one of the greatest self-promoters of the last century, and perhaps his hustle served as a model for the younger Infantile Leftists. Or was it just that all their shared attributes simply clicked in the twentieth century with the emerging worldwide media? Gandhi, the Coat-and-Tie Radicals, and later, the Infantile Leftists—they simply knew how to put on a good show for the twentieth century's newsrooms. They knew, as did Rousseau and Marx in

---

* Citations are abundant, but there is this particularly comprehensive passage in Richard Grenier's 1983 book, *The Gandhi Nobody Knows*, published in response to the movie about this colossal fraud: "I cannot honestly say I had any reasonable expectation that the film would show scenes of Gandhi's pretty teenage girl followers fighting 'hysterically' (the word was used) for the honor of sleeping naked with the Mahatma and cuddling the nude septuagenarian in their arms. (Gandhi was 'testing' his vow of chastity in order to gain moral strength for his mighty struggle with Jinnah.) When told there was a man named Freud who said that, despite his declared intention, Gandhi might actually be enjoying the caresses of the naked girls, Gandhi continued, unperturbed. Nor, frankly, did I expect to see Gandhi giving daily enemas to all the young girls in his ashrams (his daily greeting was, 'Have you had a good bowel movement this morning, sister?'), nor see the girls giving him his daily enema. Although Gandhi seems to have written less about home rule for India than he did about enemas, and excrement, and latrine cleaning ('The bathroom is a temple. It should be so clean and inviting that anyone would enjoy eating there'), I confess such scenes might pose problems for a Western director."

earlier times, what buttons to push with the *Kultursmogists*. Now, in the twenty-first century, they have run their course.

In the end, there was only one political value that the Infantile Leftists invariably stood by, never ever to have forsaken it. It is not freedom. They adore higher taxes. Their limits on free expression can be seen in their proscription of "hate speech" and their slavish advocacy of political correctness. They would regulate, tax, and proscribe anything that becomes controversial, such as tobacco, fatty foods, and gas-guzzlers. Nor are they advocates of order. They are forever weakening the police and the criminal court system. They want to relax marijuana laws and provisions against other contraband drugs. They side with the legalizers of euthanasia and other centrifugal forces in society.

What, then, is their one unvarying political value? It is to disturb the peace! They adore disturbing their neighbors' settled ways, and they do it often, as long as their neighbors remain docile. The fact is that the Infantile Leftists do not demonstrate great resolve even in disturbing the peace. They are a timorous bunch. Yet, it is amusing to contemplate that Liberalism's one political value to which all Liberals— whether zombies or otherwise—adhere, however timidly, is to disturb the peace. That is a misdemeanor in every criminal code of the civilized world. In Araby it is probably a felony.

One thing that has perplexed me is how often the Infantile Left has simply lied about both public policy and their personal persona. I mean, they have gotten caught in lies that prior generations would not even attempt. Gary Hart, the first Infantile Leftist, told petty lies about himself that he did not have to tell, and serious lies that were noteworthy for their conspicuousness. After all, it was he who challenged the media to scrutinize his after-hours recreations, and when they found him with Donna Rice, he was amazed. I cannot think of any Infantile Leftist who has not been caught shamelessly at large in false face. Even Al Gore is not exempt. He has, of late, made himself scarce, owing perhaps to our extremely cold winters and to the testimony of a masseuse (or was it several masseuses)? However, there were lies swirling about him for years: his marriage was the model of *Love Story*, he invented the Internet, and on and on.

Why are so many of the Infantile Leftists autobiographical liars and worse? It brings us back to the question of why Liberalism is dead. For a generation the modern-day theoreticians of Progressivism have advocated lying to the masses about policy, so why not also lie about one's exploits in battle (Kerry), or the origins of one's name (Hillary, creating the legend that she was named after Sir Edmund Hillary, though she was born six years before he became famous), or about almost everything, including his golf score (Bill).

The two leading theoreticians of today's Progressivism are John Rawls, who inspired scores of pedagogues throughout the nation to become what are called Deliberative Democrats, and Richard Rorty, whose work instigated a resurgence of pragmatism on college campuses, called Neopragmatism. Both professors equate Progressivism with nothing less than justice itself. It is difficult to argue against justice, and the learned gogues know it. Their sophistications permeate many of our nation's leading campuses. How deeply the Infantile Leftists have read their works, I cannot say, but there is a whiff of incense to the profs' moral superiority that Infantile Leftists also exude, to say nothing of the Stealth Socialist, Obama.

In fact, Obama's policy deceits positively reek of moral superiority, all of which come after the modern leftist's clever caveat: his decisions could not possibly represent moral superiority. After all, he has taken into account all sides. Everyone has had a say. Now the president will decide, and after that, how about a round of golf?

Cass Sunstein, at the time a professor at Harvard Law School, explained the majestic process in the January 30, 2008, *New Republic.* Obama is a "visionary minimalist." Albeit "willing to think big and to endorse significant departures from the status quo," he would "prefer to do so after accommodating, learning from, and bringing on board a variety of different perspectives."[4] Months later Sunstein returned to the topic in the September 10, 2008, *New Republic,* saying Obama "prefers solutions that can be accepted by people with a wide variety of theoretical inclinations." Obama's "skepticism about conventional ideological categories is principled, not strategic."[5] But in the end, those who disagree with him can stuff it. He knows what is best for everyone.

This kind of thinking is the thinking of a bully or an autocrat. Peter Berkowitz, in a learned disquisition on the sources of Obama's thought—and modern-day Liberalism's too—cites three sources: Rawls, Rorty, and, in the case of Obama's Supreme Court appointments, a popular law school theory, empathy.[6] They posit a superior way of arriving at a position, something like a fist to the jaw, a rifle butt to one's vulnerable organs, or a visit from the Internal Revenue Service.

Let us begin with empathy. It is a kind of halitosis of the mind that assumes a good heart and a sensitive soul. It insists that, if one can lay claim to having suffered oppression or exclusion, one has a superior insight into oppression or exclusion and almost anything else. Once one has accepted the essential premises of empathy, one cannot be argued with. A similar thought process was attributed to the lords and ladies of the Middle Ages, which in its day was a kind of eau de toilette of the mind. It assumed that a good heart and a sensitive soul could be ensured by proper breeding. Thus the insights of the lords and the ladies—as with the insights of today's certifiably oppressed or excluded—were superior and not to be argued with. Aristocracy lost its legitimacy with the rise of the philosophers of the Enlightenment and the shopkeepers. Today, empathy loses its legitimacy the farther one gets from a college campus.

As for the writing of Rawls and Rorty, their thought is mainly confined to the campus also. Both equate their thought with justice, though they could as easily equate their thought with divine inspiration. Through cerebration that amounts to sophistry—though again their thoughts could result from communing with the gods—they come to conclusions about the uses of government that they assure us would be reached by all average Americans, if average Americans had any sense at all, along with all the other admirable qualities that Rawls and Rorty insist they possess. Rawls and Rorty seem to agree with Herbert Croly, whom I quoted in chapter 2. Croly wrote in the last century, "The average American individual is morally and intellectually inadequate to a serious and consistent conception of his responsibilities as a democrat."[7] Yet Rawls and Rorty improve on Croly because they never come out and say anything so gauche. They obfuscate and advocate the higher lie.

The New Progressives led by Rawls and Rorty equate Progressive policies and goals with justice and fairness. They claim to be uniquely democratic, but those of us who love liberty and the rule of law are not so sure. We find their thinking antidemocratic and illiberal. Possibly Obama is a very good man and very wise. However, what if he gets very excited about the prospects of some stupendous good for the polity, say, universal health care. Admittedly, it will entail stripping some citizens of cherished rights should universal health care be enacted into law, but what the heck? Obama is a good disciple of Rawls and Rorty. Through high intelligence and the utmost regard for opposing points of view, he will make the smart choice. He will go ahead and establish boards that will deny health care to some citizens and grant it to others. A thirty-five-year-old gets an artificial hip, but not the sixty-five-year-old and certainly not the eighty-five-year-old. You cannot have everything. Rawls and Rorty bring us into the modern world, unrestrained by the rule of law, limited government, or the Constitution. But remember, Rawls and Rorty are dead.

Berkowitz confronts the deviousness of the New Progressives and suggests our constitutional alternative, which has the advantage of not being based on lies and, in fact, of having ensured our liberties for over two hundred years. He wrote:

> But in contrast to the original progressivism, the new progressivism seeks to obscure its awkward combination of egalitarianism and elitism.
>
> In contrast, the Constitution undertakes to reconcile the need for expert knowledge with the imperatives of

self-government through institutional design—the creation of a system of representation aimed at refining the popular will, and a separation, balancing, and blending of powers among branches of the federal government and division of power between the federal government and the state government. But the ultimate check on expertise and elites, according to the political theory on which the Constitution is based, is the people. [8]

In the Constitution there is life. There is energy. In statism there is only stagnation and death.

7

THE NUMBERS

While inspecting the body politic, one encounters one clear sign that Liberalism is dead. It is the condition of our political discourse. Polite commentators note that the dialogue is "rancorous." Some say "toxic."[1] Actually it is worse than that. The dialogue is non-existent; it is dead. From the right, from the sophisticated right, there is an attempt to engage the Liberals. I suspect we got this expectation of dialogue from the Liberals themselves when we were their students so many years ago. They were our profs, and they portrayed themselves as interested in discussing the issues of the day "with intelligent conservatives, if only they could be found."

Well, here we are, and there are a lot of us. From the Liberals, however, there is only silence. The Liberals prattle on about Glenn Beck or Sarah Palin, but they pay almost no attention to the conservatives' think tanks, to their journals of opinion, or to their writers of heft. Liberalism is at room temperature and getting colder all the time.

There are the zombies out there, the living dead. They are well-known politicians such as Al Gore or writers such as the *New York Times* columnist Paul Krugman, whom the *Wall Street Journal*'s James Taranto always playfully—but accurately—identifies as "a former Enron advisor." Yet somehow these figures on the left do not amount to much when compared with their historic predecessors. Gore flies around the country in private planes and resides in various mansions, creating the "carbon footprint" of a dinosaur. He talks about those who disagree with him as "deniers," equating them with Holocaust deniers, an ugly if typical exaggeration. In the chill of winter, he is strangely in hiding. Did yesteryear's heralds of Liberalism ever live so high on the hog (*Sus scrofa domesticus*) as Gore? Did they so shamelessly become multimillionaires from their vaticinations of doom?

Krugman howls at his opponents. He vilifies the Heritage Foundation while fudging that think tank's findings. "Whenever you encounter 'research' from the Heritage Foundation," he writes, "you always have to bear in mind that Heritage isn't really a think tank; it's a propaganda shop. Everything it says is automatically suspect. . . . Don't believe anything Heritage says."[2] Of Congressman Paul Ryan and his elaborately thought-out 2012 Budget, he joshes humorlessly, "Gosh. For a plan that supposedly sets a new standard of seriousness, Paul Ryan's vision depends an awful lot on unicorn sightings—belief in the impossible."[3] Some of Ryan's numbers did not add up. They were subsequently corrected. Still, neither Krugman nor any contemporary Liberal is capable of engaging serious conservatives in debate. When Krugman appears before a microphone, he often overheats.

The Liberals' idea of dialogue amounts to hurling what are lines fit for a bumper sticker—"I Am a Citizen of the World," "War Is Not the Answer," "Ryan Rides a Unicorn." Or perhaps they settle on a slur—conservatives are "extreme," though by now conservatives have been around for decades and running the country more frequently than not: the Reagan administration, two Bush administrations (George H. W. and George W.), and the Gingrich Congress. Liberalism has lost the trust of reasonable minds. Liberalism is dead.

There has been an odd and unanticipated change in the politically charged audience of this great Republic. Liberals once were highly intellectual. Some prided themselves in being the *only* intellectuals. In 1950 Lionel Trilling could write:

> In the United States at this time Liberalism is not only the dominant but even the sole intellectual tradition. For it is the plain fact that nowadays there are no conservative or reactionary ideas in general circulation. This does not mean, of course, that there is no impulse to conservatism or to reaction. Such impulses are certainly very

strong, perhaps even stronger than most of us know. But
the conservative impulse and the reactionary impulse do
not, with some isolated and some ecclesiastical exceptions, express themselves in ideas but only in action or in
irritable mental gestures which seek to resemble ideas.[4]

Truth be told, five years after Trilling wrote these lapi-
dary lines, William F. Buckley Jr. began *National Review*.
Now Liberalism lies beneath a cold headstone.

When I began as editor-in-chief of *The American
Spectator* four decades ago, Liberals and conservatives had
a lively dialogue. Debates took place across the country. In
fact, about thirty years ago, I began taking reader surveys of
the magazine's audience and discovered that a considerable
percentage of our audience was composed of self-described
Liberals. That is not the case today. Hardly any Liberals
wander into our audience.

What is more, thirty years ago we had Liberals participating in our symposia, reviewing books, and doing the
occasional article. One very popular annual feature of the
magazine has been our Christmas Books Issue. There we
had Liberals participating along with conservatives and
the occasional nonpolitical contributor, all suggesting liter-
ary gifts for the Yuletide season. It provided an interesting
glimpse into the minds of interesting people. David Broder
of the *Washington Post* was asked for his favorite books,

as were Governor Mario Cuomo and Father Theodore Hesburgh of Notre Dame University. They delivered. So did others. Marty Peretz of the *New Republic* contributed, as did Robert Lekachman, a contributor to the *Nation* and a well-educated, albeit left-wing, economist from City University of New York. Lekachman even did an essay for us. Daniel Patrick Moynihan famously contributed to our pages, along with his aide Penn Kemble, at the time a socialist. For a while Pat's son, Tim, did artwork. I never asked Tim his politics. It did not matter. Today it does. We rarely get Liberals to contribute to this effort.

The problem is not contained to *The American Spectator*. The American Enterprise Institute, the Heritage Foundation, the Hoover Institution, and other think tanks on the right all have the same problem. Call it the problem of One Hand Clapping. They cannot get participants from the left for their panels and other projects. They once did, but now rarely.

Sometimes I ask myself, "How did we let the Liberals down? Why are we no longer on speaking terms? Is it something we did?" In my case, I am told from a source well placed at CNN that *The Spectator* is not included in programming "because of what you did to the Clintons." What did I do to the Clintons? Was it to make fun of them? Well, they were funny. Just as Jimmy Carter was funny. That was back in the mid-1970s, and it never shut off communications with Moynihan or Lekachman or Kemble—or, in times to come, CNN. Now add Newt Gingrich to the group of politicos and eggheads whom we make fun of. Conservative show-offs can be funny, too, but I doubt that they take a joke at their expense quite as seriously as Liberals. The Liberals in their last days became very angry.

Was it the Paula Corbin Jones misunderstanding? As I have made clear through the years, Mrs. Jones's complaint was the result of an editorial oversight. We endeavored to keep the names of Clinton's liaisons out of our historic piece, which chronicled the Arkansas state troopers' revelations about their boss's sporting life with the ladies in parking lots, on the floor of the governor's mansion, occasionally in a rented bed. One lapse—it was the piece's writer, David Brock, I believe, who was responsible for it—left the beauteous Paula's first name exposed (only her first name). Somehow she found out (though she never was a big reader) and sued Bill for sexual harassment. In due course, he was asked, under oath, the particulars of his relationships with certain women. He, of course, lied about them, but he *obviously* lied about his trysts with that loquacious bombshell Monica Lewinsky. Scientific tests proved beyond any reasonable doubt that he lied. *He* lied, not *The Spectator*. Ironically, Bill was always a big supporter of sexual harassment law; I have always thought the law impractical. He brought the impeachment down on himself. I am innocent.

Yet, if Troopergate explains why the Liberals distance themselves from our pages, it does not explain why the Liberals distance themselves from other conservative organizations. Or for that matter, it does not explain their reluctance to read the magazine, perhaps for some fugitive delight, as reading the memoirs of Giovanni Jacopo Casanova might be a delight for them, or certain lewd passages from *Das Kapital*. Nor does it explain why they never attempt to establish dialogue with the right, not even with Glenn Beck, not even with the pulchritudinous Sarah Palin.

Something else has changed among the Liberals. I think that the reason the Liberals have avoided contact with the right—even fleeting symposia, even a letter to the editor—is that for decades they have been losing to conservatism in an obvious but very troubling way: the numbers. Perhaps, they do not exactly acknowledge their slippage, but even the most obtuse get the feeling that *something* has changed. Is it the emergence of talk radio? Is it the terrible specter of Glenn Beck? Well, Liberals are the ones that are horrified by him. Why do they not move on and engage, say, Thomas Sowell, or if they must watch TV and it has to be Fox News, Brit Hume?

One of the last areas in which they still have influence is in the area of public discourse, and all they do is caterwaul about its "toxicity."[5] Well, improve it. Engage in public discourse with intelligent minds. Unfortunately, there is no response. It is hopeless.

In part Liberals do not engage because they cannot. There are no Moynihans or Lekachmans remaining, and certainly no Hubert Humphreys or Adlai Stevensons. The intelligent left is almost nonexistent, and what left there is does not want to be exposed by the right's analysis. We conservatives are steeped in their writing. *The American Spectator, National Review,* the *Weekly Standard,* to say nothing of the *Wall Street Journal,* often comment on Liberal arguments and diatribes, but from the other side there is generally silence.

They remain distant from conservatism, primly maligning conservatives as radical or extreme—terms that were plausible enough in the early 1950s but now are positively antique. They will control their TV shows, their cable outlets, the struggling *Kultursmog.* They take refuge in their think tanks, in their newsrooms, and in their university faculties. At National Public Radio they had one intelligent moderate, Juan Williams. He spoke freely and credibly, and they fired him.

The consequences are vast. Not only does the left not engage in dialogue with the right. The Liberals' blah-blah-blah has gaping holes in it. The holes are empirically observable and difficult for them to explain. The Liberals are forever holding forth on the fragmentation or exhaustion of the right. They, in their presumption, offer helpful hints on how conservatism can still be constructive and avoid further setbacks. By contrast, conservatives *never* offer similar helpful hints to Liberals. Why this is, I shall not hazard a guess. Possibly we on the right unconsciously realize that the Liberals are too far gone for resuscitation. Possibly, we do not give a damn. At any rate, the Liberals have for years offered conservatives revitalizing advice that usually amounts to a several-step program toward becoming Liberals or perhaps toward retirement from politics altogether. Conservatives are to be contented with paying taxes and nothing more.

In 2006 many writers of the Liberal persuasion noted the conservatives' decline in the polls and tendered the diagnosis that conservatism had become "exhausted," "fragmented," or "cracked-up."[6] Only in 2008, when things got worse for conservatives, did one bold fellow come forward and volunteer his services as our final obituarist, writing a whole book, *The Death of Conservatism*. He was Sam Tanenhaus. The imp edited the *New York Times Book Review* and simultaneously the *Times'* influential "Week in Review" section. What he does in his leisure hours, I have yet to discern. Possibly he drives a pedicab in Central Park with his baseball hat on backwards.

His charmless opuscule began as an essay in the February 18, 2009, number of the *New Republic*, "Conservatism Is Dead: An Intellectual Autopsy." Yet it caused so much excitement—at least among Liberals—that by the end of the year, it appeared in book form and was available everywhere.* At the time, however, there was a problem: the numbers.

According to the Gallup poll's annual average on ideological identification at the end of 2009, conservatives outnumbered Liberals by 40 percent to 21 percent, with moderates weighing in at 35 percent (see Chart 1). For the Pew Research Center, the responses were similar. In November 2009, 36 percent in a Pew Research Center survey called themselves conservatives, 34 percent moderates, 21 percent Liberal. Even in a Democratic year, 2008, the Harris Interactive's compilation had conservatives outnumbering Liberals 37 percent to 18 percent, with 41 percent weighing in as moderates (see chart 2). Why did Tanenhaus not tell us about these numbers? Other polls have been pretty much in agreement, at least in terms of trending. Where would there ever be enough coffins to bury our dead? What was going to happen to our think tanks, our publications, and our university chairs? Whatever would happen to Fox News? Would it take over for American Geographic TV? *Is* there an American Geographic TV?

---

* There was another similarly funereal effort. The book, supposedly written by James Carville, was *40 More Years: How Democrats Will Rule the Next Generation*. Copies of it are difficult to acquire. One hears of book burners incinerating books that they fear or otherwise disrelish. This book was burned by Carville's friends and admirers. It vanished from their bookshelves. They sought to protect his reputation as a sage. Their effort was futile.

Chart 1. Gallup: Ideological Identification, 1992–2010

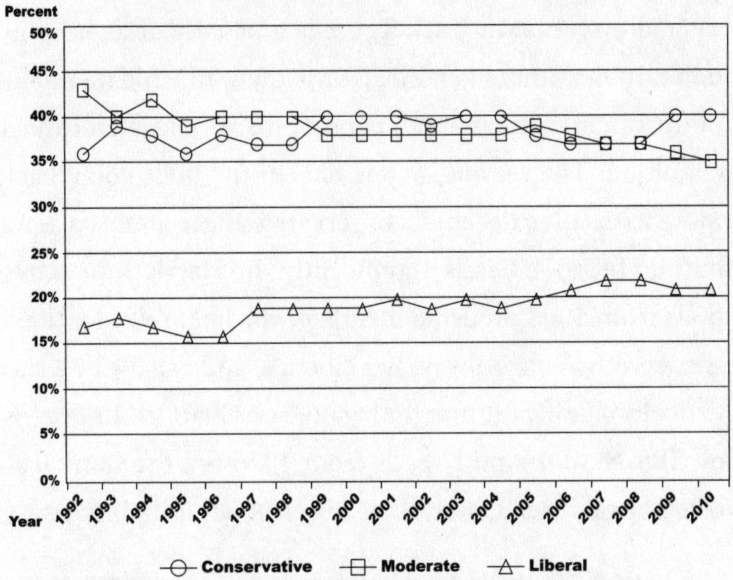

Percent

Question asked is: How would you describe your political views—very conservative, moderate, liberal, or very liberal? Source: Gallup

Tanenhaus's book reads like a graduate student's research paper in intellectual history, even engaging in pointless speculation. He had very nice things to say about certain conservatives, but they were all dead. Edmund Burke was mentioned, and William F. Buckley Jr. In a proper response to Tanenhaus's speculations, one might say *maybe*. Maybe Burke, if alive today, would oppose gun control, and maybe he would not. Maybe Buckley would be very disappointed in Sarah Palin, or maybe he would ask her for a date.

Who knows how this insufferable grad student's speculations about these conservative giants might turn out, and who cares? However, let me say that I doubt his perspicacity and even his sincerity. There is a paucity of data in his book. In fact, there is none. Nor is there much data in any of the other writings about conservatism's alleged terminal condition. The reason is apparent. In the polls going back more than three decades, conservatives have almost always outnumbered Liberals significantly. In Harris Interactive polls from 1968 on using identical wording, self-identified conservatives have always led Liberals, and usually by a statistically significant margin (again, see Chart 2). In dozens of CBS News monthly polls from 1976 on, the same pattern appears (see Chart 3). Gallup has published its yearly

Chart 2. The Harris Poll: Ideological Identification, 1968–2008

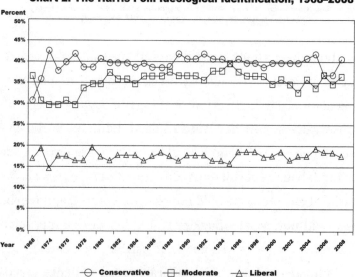

Question asked is: How do you describe your own political philosophy—conservative, moderate, or liberal? Source: Surveys by Harris Interactive.

averages from 2000, and each year conservatives have out-numbered Liberals (again, see Chart 1). That conservatives are fragile and forever in danger of disappearing is another Liberal delusion. Conservatives have grown in numbers, and Liberals have stagnated.

Chart 3. CBS News: Ideological Identification 1976–2010

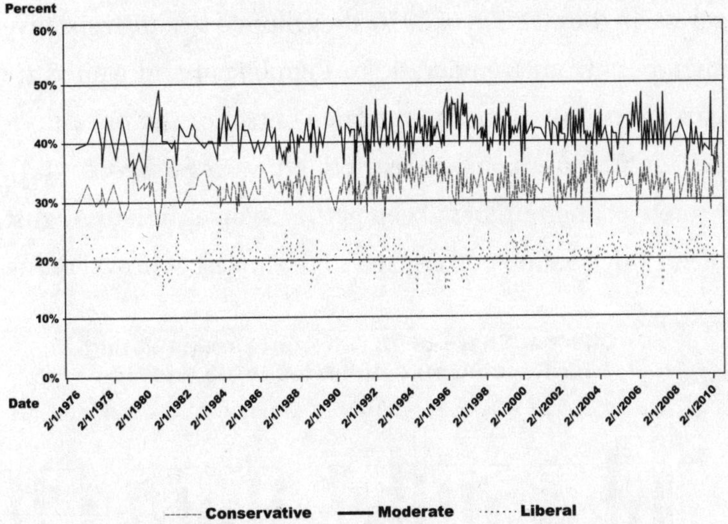

Question asked is: How would you describe your views on most political matters? Generally do you think of yourself as liberal, moderate, or conservative?

I estimate that today there are more bird-watchers than Liberals in America, and possibly more nudists. If trends continue there will indubitably be more nude bird-watchers. Perhaps the day will come when nude bird-watchers and Liberals can hold joint maneuvers. The requisite charts and graphs will be made available in this book's subsequent editions.

The problem is that among the citizenry, conservatives always outnumber the Liberals, and now in some surveys they outnumber the moderates. The moderates and conservatives have, in truth, been under assault by Liberal programs for years, and they are now reasserting themselves. In the election of 2010, they flipped twenty legislative chambers from Democratic to Republican and gained six governorships. With them came control of the once-in-a-decade Congressional redistricting process[7] (see Chart 4). Moreover the numbers keep getting worse. In late August of 2011 the Gallup poll registered the lowest approval rating

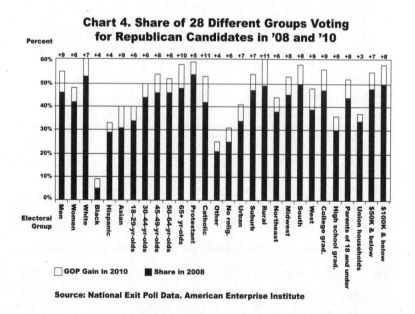

Chart 4. Share of 28 Different Groups Voting for Republican Candidates in '08 and '10

GOP Gain in 2010   Share in 2008

Source: National Exit Poll Data. American Enterprise Institute

for the federal government since the poll began, 17 percent positive, 63 percent(!) negative, and a net approval rating of −46 percent (yes, *minus* 46 percent!). The federal government was supposed to be the Liberals' magic wand for returning us to the happy land of the New Deal!

It does not look good for Liberalism. Conservatives and moderates are in agreement that they face exorbitant taxes from the Democrats and budgetary overhang that will change the nature of our government's relation to the citizenry. Even on abortion most conservatives and a sizable number of moderates are in agreement that it is wrong. Other social issues, too, unite them. From 2006 on, the Democrats have overreached. Now conservatives and moderates want their freedoms and their bank accounts back. They know that the Democrats profligate spending has entered historically unprecedented regions of 25 percent of GDP. All they want is to get it down to where Ronald Reagan had it. From the assembled charts we see that the numbers do not favor the Liberals and have not favored them for years. We live in a democracy, not a plutocracy.

In 2010 the Liberals admonished against the Tea Party's many supposed excesses. Yet, 41 percent of the electorate actually identified with the Tea Party. The Tea Partiers became a very significant bloc of voters in that election. From 2008 to the historic election of 2010, the GOP gained ground in virtually every electoral category (again, see Chart 4).

Also in 2010, 35 percent of the vote was white working class (defined as not having finished college). Sixty-three percent of them voted with the Republicans, leaving 33 percent of the white working class to vote Democratic.[8] In 2008, when 39 percent of the voters were from the white working class, they had voted Republican by ten percentage points.[9] But in 2010 they switched massively to the GOP, voting for the Republicans by a full thirty points. This shift cannot be ignored.

The white working class believes in the country. They are suspicious of elites. They do not like radical change, left or right. They now feel that the Liberals have deserted them, leaving them behind economically and in terms of respect. Remember candidate Obama's 2008 quote about voters who "cling to guns or religion or antipathy to people who aren't like them"? He was talking in large part about these voters, apparently oblivious that they provided the bedrock for the New Deal, the New Frontier, and the Great Society.[10] Perhaps he never knew it. Yet now, increasingly the white working class votes with the Republicans. Nothing Obama has said or done has won these voters back. He is engaged in class warfare, but without the largest component of the working class.

Up until recent years the Liberals, through their control of the *Kultursmog*, have been able to characterize issues and candidates in any way they wanted. In a 1970 interview with the journalist Theodore White, George McGovern, then quietly taking over the Democratic Party with the most radical reorganizing program ever, was careful to dissemble to White that he was no "ideologue . . . not a Barry Goldwater."[11] Even then McGovern, in 1948 a Wallaceite and now intent on radical reform, had an eye out for the *Kultursmog*. He was about to proceed with the most radical campaign in American history, but he had to observe the false pieties of the *smog*. So he took a swat at Goldwater, and both he and the keepers of the *Kultursmog* hoped the electorate could be conned. The voters beat him soundly in 1972, but in the *smog* his false claim to moderation has endured. There, in that sacrosanct ether, Goldwater, the 1968 herald of Reaganism, is the ideologue; McGovern, the radical of 1972, is the innocent who probably had the election stolen from him by the unscrupulous Richard Nixon. In many ways the *Kultursmog* has served as Disneyland for adults.

Yet today there are objections to the *Kultursmog's* deceits. There is an alternative point of view holding the Liberals accountable. Now through Fox News,[12] talk radio, the Internet, and various organs of opinion and newspapers on the right, the citizenry can choose between the candidates and the policies of the left and the right. No wonder the Liberals are not talking to the right. Everyone can now listen in, and at least a significant number of journalists in the media will tell you that in the White House today there sits a Stealth Socialist. However, today President Barack

Obama's stealth is futile; conservatives and moderates are wise to his act. That is the cause of the Liberals' anger. Their stealth, and for that matter, McGovern's, is no longer a secret. For that matter the *Kultursmog* now stands exposed.

8

. . . AND WHAT COMES NEXT

Two and a half years ago, with our country on the edge of a second Great Depression, we met with the president in the White House to discuss whether to move in those first months of his administration to legislate fundamental reform of the financial system—or wait until we had put the crisis behind us.

The president made two key decisions. First, he chose to move forward, knowing that the forces of opposition to reform would grow stronger as the memory of the crisis receded. And second, he asked us to write draft legislation rather than propose broad principles. The president did not want the new rules to end up being written by those who brought us to the edge of catastrophic financial failure.

In June 2009, the administration submitted to Congress a proposal that would fundamentally reshape the financial system. It was designed to lay a stronger foundation for innovation, economic growth and job creation with robust protections for consumers and investors and tough constraints on risk-taking. We drew on ideas and insights from reform-oriented thinkers across the political spectrum.[1]

—TIMOTHY GEITHNER,
Wall Street Journal
July 20, 2011

The nation has arrived at a great reckoning. That strange and meretricious ideology that came to power in the New Deal, then episodically waxed and waned in the New Frontier and the Great Society, and self-destructively waxed yet again in the first years of the Prophet Obama, is dead. The sad expiry was a long time in coming.

For some sixty-five years it dominated our *Kultur* out of all proportion to its numbers, but now the *Kultursmog,* too, is fizzling. Liberalism's ghastly zombies have haunted our politics, but in constantly dwindling numbers. In government bureaucracies Liberalism's living dead are more secure, but the fate of those bureaucracies is in doubt. At any rate, ever since the creation of huge government bureaucracies in the faraway time of Otto von Bismarck, bureaucrats have shown an aptitude for changing their colors. As a group, they are the original chameleons on plaid. James Piereson, always a keen political observer, and others have written that the bureaucratic zombies will keep the

Liberal project going.[2] I doubt it. Most of them will adapt to the next orthodoxy.

Yet, though Liberalism is dead, the enormous cost it racked up will lay heavy on the Republic for years to come, long after the last Liberal has been interred in Forest Lawn Memorial Cemetery along with some forlorn Hollywoodian's other household pets—I see Al Gore interred alongside Barbra Streisand's cockatoo. The budgetary deficits we are facing are staggering, and the federal government's level of indebtedness is worse. More subtly, our freedoms and our constitutional form of government are making heavy weather of it. Fortunately the public has turned to the Constitution, and it is the Constitution that is the antidote to Liberalism and to what might come after.

The notion of Liberalism's demise is spreading through the conservative intelligentsia, as is the sense that our refuge is to be found in the American Constitution. Tea Partiers and moderates, also known as independents, are joining with all the earlier recruits of conservatism—the Neoconservatives, the Reagan Democrats, the evangelicals or the religious right—to share the sense that something on the American political scene is no more, and that something that was there at the Founding remains to serve the citizenry again, the Constitution.

On the eve of July 4, 2011, Victor Davis Hanson, a senior fellow at the Hoover Institution, wrote in *National Review*

Online his version of Liberalism's lifeless condition. "This Fourth of July," he said, "what remains is the Founders' vision of a limited government; the idea of a population united by common values, themes, and ideas; a republican form of checks-and-balances government to prevent demagoguery, factions, and tyranny of the majority; the sanctity and autonomy of the nation-state; and individual freedom and liberty as protected through the Bill of Rights. Everything after and against that has proved a failure." Liberalism is dead.

Hanson, who as a military historian and classics professor has published widely, went on to perform his autopsy on the corpse. "Indeed," he wrote, "what makes this Fourth different from recent celebrations is the ongoing repudiation of almost everything antithetical to the Founders' views—the redistributive, all-powerful welfare state, the therapeutic arrogance that believes human nature can be altered by an omnipotent well-meaning government, the postmodern notion that nationhood and borders are passé, and the utopian idea that war can be declared obsolete and the need for defense transcended. From Greece to California such dreams are dead [that word again!]."

He offers a cursory prognosis: "Here in the United States, we await the imposition of Obamacare, despite the fact that the public does not want it, the nation cannot afford it, politicians regret it, and companies seek exemption from it. Our current pace of $1.6 trillion annual deficits, for all the talk of Keynesian gymnastics, is unsustainable—and even acknowledged as such by those who are most responsible for the latest round of fiscal irresponsibility. As we near fifty million Americans on food stamps, another year of 9-plus percent unemployment, and the third $1 trillion-plus budget deficit, even statists are beginning to see that statism does not work."[3] On that last matter I think Victor goes over the top. The statists cannot renounce statism, as they never announced it. It was another of their stealth endeavors. Moreover, they are zombies, or "Frankensteins" as Victor calls them. They have been bereft of new ideas since about the time Eleanor Roosevelt adopted the new idea of "airing" her children. Liberalism is dead.

So what comes after it? Well, you recall that Liberalism sprang from Progressivism, which promised that society was about to be administered by the Best Minds while the rest of us scratched our poor noodles and tried to master their higher thoughts. Then Progressivism quietly melded into Liberalism and became part of Liberalism's confused heritage until its First Civil War, when one of the tough-minded Liberals, Irwin Ross, included scraps of it in his *Strategy for Liberals*. In that book Ross described, rather muzzy-headedly, a future America that would feature a "mixed economy" under the direction of a strong Progressive movement. Without being Communist, fascist, or socialist, Ross's mixed economy would have gobbled up vast sectors of the economy, which would nonetheless remain free, mainly because he said it would. Actually his scheme for the future took up pieces of socialism, fascism, and contemporary Liberalism, just as the New Deal had. Ever the manipulator of ideas, this gifted Liberal then camouflaged these authoritarian tendencies under the dulcet term *liberalism*, or as I say, *Liberalism*.

Like a vast camorra, the government would act in league with the Giant Corporations and banking interests to produce goods and services intelligently, steadily, and now, in the twenty-first century, presumably in the green way, without deep recessions or any other inconvenient events. The trade unions, the fat cats, and various other interest groups would all work together with the Best Minds in human harmony.

Looking back on it, we see that something like this was tried by President Barack Obama in the first years of his presidency. His first chief of staff, Rahm Emanuel, announced bloodlessly Obama's great departure to a gathering of corporate titans at a *Wall Street Journal* conference shortly after the 2008 election. "You never want a serious crisis to go to waste," pronounced Emanuel. Actually, I doubt that even he knew what was coming, for surely he would not have been so cavalier about policies that would lead to millions of Americans being unemployed and millions more being mired in a low-growth economy.

It all began when the government took over AIG, Chrysler, General Motors, and banks that were deemed "too big to fail." That was government overreach and bad policy from the Bush administration, but what came next under Obama was the spectacular expansion of the afore-mentioned government takeovers plus Obamacare and the Dodd-Frank Act. Obamacare placed one-sixth of the econ-omy under federal control, turning much of it into a kind of highly regulated public utility. Then, with the passage of the Dodd-Frank Act, the government presumed to take over practically anything that some federal bureaucracy set its sights on. Through thousands of regulations, trillions of dollars of subsidies, and outright government control, eager government bureaucrats and compliant corporate executives tried to improve upon the markets. It was regu-lation that rendered businesses the wards of the state, while leaving them in ostensibly private hands. Friedrich Hayek would have identified it as "the Road to Serfdom."[4]

The result was nearly 9-plus percent unemployment—the longest period of such high unemployment since the Depression. In fact, this recession was the longest reces-sion since the Depression, and when the economy began to grow again, its growth was anemic. It has all been a grave disappointment to the zombies, but not, I believe, to the Stealth Socialist. He has seen the future, and it is Europe. He envisages America like Scandinavia, though more diverse. Our AA+ bond rating bothers him not at all. We deserve it, he thinks.

What comes next if the lifeless Liberals ever resurrect is the Corporate State, or as those with a sense of history might call it, Friendly Fascism. Around 1980 a man of the left, Bertram Gross, actually spoke of America heading for Friendly Fascism, but he saw it as a conservative phenomenon, and it caused him grave anxiety. In truth, as we have seen, most American conservatives are au fond American constitutionalists. Their mix of libertarian values, the rule of law, and the Constitution's blend of checks and balances and federalism makes fascism anathema to them.

The real specter of Friendly Fascism was adumbrated in the crony capitalism that we saw in the first three years of our Stealth Socialist, Barack Obama, with ever-larger sectors of the economy coming under government control. Socialism and fascism are not that different. Both disregard property rights, and both rule through bureaucracy. Though fascists tend to wear uniforms, some of which are very smart, socialists have greater direct control of their bureaucracies. If one thinks that a socialist cannot become a fascist, I would suggest following the late Benito Mussolini back to his origins as a lowly socialist schoolteacher; whereupon, as time passed, *il Duce* became a dictator. The blueprint for the future of the American left, if it can ever resurrect, is fascism with a friendly face.

Fortunately President Obama is so incompetent and tone-deaf to democratic politics that I predict his immediate future will be spent building a presidential library somewhere in Blue Island, Illinois, or, in the unlikely event he is reelected, hiding from Republican majorities in both houses of Congress. If American conservatives play their hand right, Friendly Fascism will go down as an unrealized American nightmare.

Americans have since the Reagan years become accustomed to vibrant economic growth, not the European model of slow growth burdened with the high taxes and onerous regulation that Friendly Fascism—Obama's corporatism—portends. Its constituent elements were there years ago, but to all the unfunded entitlements that America faced in 2008, Obama piled on still more trillions of debt. Then he stubbornly demanded that we raise taxes, at first on those making $250,000 or more annually, but inevitably everyone would get walloped.

A review of the growth of government debt will reveal how we got to the Obama Renaissance. At the end of the Reagan administration, the accumulated national debt held by the public amounted to 41 percent of GDP. In 2008, even given George W. Bush's fiscal extravagance, it was only 40.3 percent of GDP. By the end of fiscal 2011, it was estimated at 72 percent of GDP, and by the end of 2021 the estimate is 76 percent of GDP. By then we shall be fully $18.2 trillion in hock if nothing is done. As for the combined publicly owned debt and intergovernmental debt, that reached 100 percent of GDP by 2010.

We arrived at this unhappy condition mainly because of entitlements. They began in the New Deal with Social Security, but for decades the costs were manageable. Then in the mid-1960s came Lyndon B. Johnson's Great Society with a newly confected right, the right to health care. Medicare and Medicaid were born in 1965. The estimated costs were always understated because few people understood that the demand for health care is elastic; if it is relatively cheap and people have the time to avail themselves of it, the demand will go up exponentially. The program for retirees, Medicare, was estimated to cost no more than $12 billion by 1990. It cost $110 billion. The program for the poor, Medicaid, was worse. It has grown from $4 billion in 1966, to $41 billion in 1986, to $243 billion in 2010—in large part thanks to the expanded eligibility vouchsafed by thoughtless congresspersons.

Other entitlements presented themselves. Public housing, rent supplements, food stamps, day care, home-heating assistance, sex therapy, and more—all unfunded. By 2010 the federal government was spending approximately $20,000 for every man, woman, and child living in poverty, according to the great authority on government welfare policies, Robert Rector of the Heritage Foundation. By then Social Security, owing to the decline of its support base (according to the

Congressional Budget Office, the ratio of workers to beneficiaries fell from 4.9 in 1960 to 2.8 in 2010) and to trillions of dollars of additional unfunded liabilities, was 20 percent of the federal budget and headed for bankruptcy in 2037. It is already beginning to pay out more in benefits than it collects in revenue. By 2011, 50.5 million Americans were on Medicaid, 46.5 million on Medicare, 52 million on Social Security, 44.6 million on food stamps, along with lesser numbers of recipients on Supplemental Security Income and unemployment insurance. In 2011 there were 26 million Americans receiving earned-income tax credit. By 2010 such payments accounted for over 70 percent of the federal budget, an increase from 28 percent in 1965 (see Chart 5).

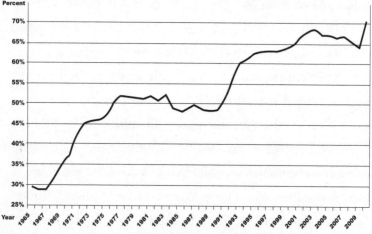

Chart 5. Percent of Federal Spending on Entitlements, 1965–2010
Payments to Dependent Individuals as a Percentage of Federal Outlays

Source: Office of Management and Budget, and Heritage Foundation Calculations

By then President Obama had incipiently introduced Friendly Fascism. Federal spending as a share of GDP was higher than at any time since World War II. From some 20 percent of GDP it climbed to a historically unheard-of peacetime percentage of 25 (see Chart 6), and our forty-fourth president wanted to keep it there until he could expand it again. In his first three years in office, the debt was increased by more than $4 trillion, and that did not include his Obamacare entitlement that envisaged thirty million more Americans on government health care. He claimed his spending was necessary to deal with the Great Recession, but it prolonged the recession, creating uncertainty in the

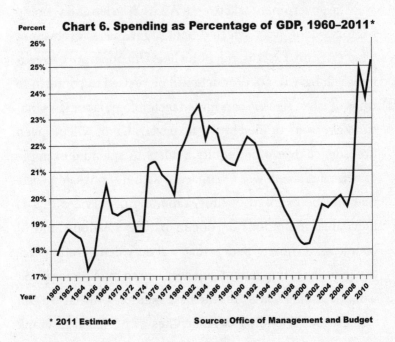

Percent   **Chart 6. Spending as Percentage of GDP, 1960–2011***

* 2011 Estimate   Source: Office of Management and Budget

markets and hobbling growth. By 2011 he had a growth rate of 1.3 percent, as against Ronald Reagan's 7.1 percent at about the same time in Reagan's recovery cycle. Obama's unemployment numbers hovered at 9-plus percent, and the debt was appalling. But he still spoke elliptically of raising taxes, which would have to be raised to as much as 60 percent, 70 percent, or even 80 percent to finance his projects and promises. His presidency presaged a whole new model for American society breaking with the recent past and with the Founding Fathers' vision. It would be Friendly Fascism but without the uniforms and the marching bands, only the Internal Revenue Service and various other federal agencies.

The government takeover of AIG, Chrysler, and General Motors, along with selected banks, gave us a foretaste of what Friendly Fascism might be like. Uncooperative executives will have to go. Products will be revised to conform to trendy tastes: electric cars, green technology, labor laws that suit Labor—all funded by the taxpayers. Labor will be given precedence over other equity holders. A splendid example of what lies ahead was Obamacare with its concealed costs that will be exposed in time, rationing of services that is inevitable, limitations on doctor-patient relations, and of course, government panels that will defy democratic practice in order to implement policies favored by elites, or if you will, the Ruling Class. Yet the best example of what we can expect from Friendly Fascism comes with the Dodd-Frank

Act. Ostensibly a plan to reform Wall Street, it goes well beyond the Street.

We began this chapter with Timothy Geithner's sly defense of the Act in the *Wall Street Journal* and his miscasting of its rationale. As an aside allow me to remind you that Geithner was not the only Obama appointee nominated for high office only to be revealed as a tax evader. There was also former senator Tom Daschle and former mayor of Dallas Ron Kirk, among lesser wretches. It took the administration enormous arrogance to proceed with Geithner's nomination as the reformer of Wall Street, but then it took enormous arrogance to name the bill Dodd-Frank. Senator Christopher Dodd and Congressman Barney Frank, erstwhile chairman of the House Financial Services Committee, were the chief supporters and protectors on the Hill of Fannie Mae and Freddie Mac. They also supported the government policies that created the real estate bubble that led to the eventual financial meltdown. Then they, with the utmost chutzpah, applied themselves to what became Dodd-Frank, the bill to reform Wall Street and to gobble up heretofore-unimagined areas of the private sector. Friendly Fascism never looked so cynical.

We can thank Peter Wallison, the Arthur F. Burns Fellow in Financial Policy Studies at the American Enterprise Institute, for doing the scholarly excavation of this alarming specimen of Friendly Fascism. The Dodd-Frank Wall

Street Reform and Consumer Protection Act shares many qualities with the aforementioned government takeovers of the economy, not the least of which is that its enabling legislation is so voluminous that there cannot be but a handful of Capitol Hill whiz kids who actually read it. It is 2,300 pages long! Dodd-Frank's preeminent theme, says Wallison, is fear of change and of innovation. He served on the Financial Crisis Inquiry Commission (FCIC), dissenting from its findings. The Democratic-dominated Commission blamed the financial crisis on lax regulation, Wall Street greed, and failed risk-management at banks and other financial firms. Wallison sees the crisis as caused by government housing policy and faulty regulation already put in place. A growing list of experts is siding with him.

Following the Democrats' fictional narrative, Dodd-Frank prescribes a series of burdensome, bank-like regulations that would suppress change in the largest financial institutions and that would eventually run through much of our economy. What would be lost are the competitiveness, innovation, and risk-taking that have always characterized U.S. financial firms. The regulators would govern much of our financial community. The worst outcome of Dodd-Frank (and of Friendly Fascism in general) is that the vast power of federal regulation will change the nature of our financial system, rendering it a closely regulated series of utilities, subject to immutability and corruption. Now financial firms that once focused on beating the competition will focus on currying favor with government regulators, who will control them and the system in general. The regulators will answer to no one, certainly not to Congress.

What will ultimately emerge is a pact between the largest financial institutions and federal regulators—in particular, the Federal Reserve Board—with the Fed protecting these big institutions from the competition of lesser institutions and from failure. The big institutions will be the handmaidens of government policies and government directions. In addition, the newly created Consumer Financial and Protections Bureau (CFPB) will act in complete independence from Congress. The principle of Congressional control of a government bureaucracy will be lost. Congress will completely lose its oversight of an agency of the executive branch. In Wallison's words, Dodd-Frank "looks to be the most troubling—maybe even destructive—single piece of financial legislation ever adopted."[5] That is what is to be expected from Friendly Fascism.

As mentioned previously, the financial crisis began not with Wall Street but with a real estate bubble. Pursuant to government policy to get low-income individuals into the real estate market, first the Clinton administration and then the Bush administration created what grew to be

27 million subprime mortgages (by 2008, half of all mortgages), which were bundled in with healthy mortgages,
and the resulting indigestible sausages were sold throughout the American financial system and eventually around
the world. That is where Wall Street came in.* When the
bubble popped, such firms as Fannie Mae, Freddie Mac,
Bear Stearns, and Lehman Brothers suffered the conse-
quent stress. An additional problem was the accounting
practice of "mark to market," which caused such institutions to be forced to come up with more collateral when
their established collateral's value was marked down
according to book value, whether the collateral was to be
sold or not. Some institutions went down in flames, and
the government-backed institutions, Fannie and Freddie,
went hat in hand to the taxpayer.

Government regulators had failed in their duties. Now
Dodd-Frank envisages a vast extension of their duties. The
Act, which ignored the true cause of the financial crisis,
came up with still more regulations that would eventually
spread government control of markets throughout the
economy. Wallison sees the Consumer Financial Protection

---

* A timely book, *Reckless Endangerment* by Gretchen Morgenson and Joshua
Rosner (New York: Times Books, 2011), has nailed down the origins of the financial crisis. "Under Johnson," the authors wrote on page 10, referring to Fannie
Mae's chairman, the Democratic operative James A. Johnson, "Fannie Mae led the
way in encouraging loose lending practices among banks whose loans the company bought. . . . Johnson led both the private and public sectors down the path
that led directly to the financial crisis of 2008."

Bureau (CFPB) set up by Dodd-Frank as probably having "the widest reach into the U.S. economy of any agency in Washington. Although some people seem to imagine it is just an independent agency to regulate how banks treat their customers, it has much broader jurisdiction than that."[6] Using material compiled by Davis-Polk, a New York–based law firm, he elaborates. In so doing he has charted another example of what comes after Liberalism—Friendly Fascism—in this instance, the control of much of the American economy. Here are some examples of what Dodd-Frank covers:

Extending credit and servicing loans, including acquiring, purchasing, selling, brokering, or other extensions of credit;

Extending or brokering leases of personal or real property that are the functional equivalent of purchase finance arrangements;

Engaging in deposit-taking activities, transmitting or exchanging funds, or otherwise acting as a custodian of funds or any financial instruments for use by or on behalf of a consumer;

Providing most real estate settlement services, or performing appraisals of real estate or personal property;

Providing or issuing stored value or payment instruments, or selling such instruments, but only if the seller exercises substantial control over the terms or conditions of the stored value provided to the customer;

Providing check cashing, check collection or check guarantee services;

Providing payments or other financial data processing products or services to a consumer by any technological means;

Providing financial advisory services to consumers on individual financial matters or relating to proprietary financial products or services, including providing consumer credit counseling or services to assist consumers with debt management, debt settlement services, modifying the terms of a loan or avoiding foreclosure;

Collecting, analyzing, maintaining, or providing consumer reports or other account information, including information related to consumer credit histories, used or expected to be used in connection with any decision regarding the offering or provision of a consumer financial product or service, subject to exceptions; and

Collecting debt related to any consumer financial product or service.[7]

As with Obamacare, so with the Consumer Financial Protection Bureau; it has been set up as another inchoate institution of Friendly Fascism. It will exact costs from the economy, causing slow growth. It will stifle innovation and eliminate small business. But what is perhaps worse, in Wallison's opinion, "it will operate independently, without any control by the Fed, Congress, or the president. The DFA [Dodd-Frank Act] states that even though the CFPB [Consumer Financial Protection Bureau] is lodged in the Fed, it is not subject to the control of the Fed."[8]

There have always been authoritarian currents in Progressivism, the New Deal, and Liberalism. Of course, there are authoritarian currents in socialism and most emphatically in fascism. In the future, if there were to be a future for Liberalism, the fascism would come out. If elected to a second term and given majorities in the House and the Senate, President Obama will mutate from the Stealth Socialist to the Stealth Fascist, but I doubt his future will be in politics. Liberalism is dead.

The repudiation of the Democrats at the polls in 2010 was felt at every level of government. In Washington the Democrats suffered their greatest rout in the House since 1946, and the Republicans picked up six seats in the Senate, almost taking control of that chamber. In 2012 they will. Across the country Democrats lost over seven hundred state legislative seats. It was the largest reversal ever. As a result they lost control of twenty state chambers to the Republicans. The numbers are against the zombies. They are outnumbered two to one by conservatives, and when we throw in the moderates, or independents as they are called, it gets worse. Americans do not like Friendly Fascism. They do not even like corporate cronyism. President Obama is dead in the water.

9

PRESIDENT BARACK OBAMA, LIBERALISM'S PALLBEARER

C hairman Mao made the following statement to Edgar Snow on April 30, 1971, in an interview that he hoped would reach the ears of American policy-makers. In it he said:

> China should learn from the way America developed, by decentralizing and spreading responsibility and wealth among the 50 states. A central government could not do everything. China must depend upon regional and local initiative. It would not do [*spreading his hands*] to leave everything up to him [Mao].[1]

Forty years later, China was on the brink of becoming the world's largest economy, and President Barack Obama had not a clue about learning "from the way America developed" or about depending on its "regional and local initiatives." He was lost in the sublime quiddities of his incomparable colleagues from the Ruling Class. That would be the yokels back at academe, drunk on their higher knowledge of "how-to" studies: how to teach (education departments), how to think and analyze (psychology and sociology departments), how to administer and govern (variations of the John F. Kennedy School of Government at Harvard State University)—all the trendy "studies" offered by the modern-day multiversity or whatever they now call it. Obama does not have very many classically educated university graduates to call on. In fact, he does not have many educated people to call on.

Obama has been called many things. He is "the Anointed One" to Sean Hannity and Mark Levin, and "the Messiah" to Rush Limbaugh. He is "the Prophet" to others, myself included. Stanley Kurtz knows him as the "Stealth Socialist," and as I have argued in the previous chapter, the case can be made for calling him America's first "Stealth Fascist." Obama himself has admitted, "I know more about policies on any particular issue than my policy directors. And I'll tell you right now that I'm . . . a better political director than my political director."[2] A less emotionally involved source is presidential historian Michael Beschloss, who pronounced Obama "a guy whose IQ is off the charts," backing that judgment up with "He's probably the smartest guy ever to become president."[3]

This modest appraisal of the intellect of probably the worst president in modern times has been enough to inspire the Liberal intelligentsia to elevate him to the pantheon of modern presidential greats with Franklin D. Roosevelt and John F. Kennedy and whoever else sets their hearts aflutter. After all, he won a Nobel Prize just nine months into his presidency and wrote a sublime memoir, and have you seen his jump shot?

Yet no one has called him a pallbearer. Some might have thought that the columnist David Brooks was about to call him one when he remarked on Obama's "perfectly creased pant." A pallbearer with a well-creased pair of pants is a must, but no, David had other things in mind. The occasion was the *New York Times* columnist's first interview with the junior senator from Illinois. Brooks had just made the implausible point that Obama "knew *both* [policy and political philosophy] better than me." Then he went on to Obama's "perfectly creased pant." "I remember distinctly," said the scribe, "an image—we were sitting on his couches, and I was looking at his pant leg and his perfectly creased pant, and I'm thinking, a) he's going to be president and b) he'll be a very good president."[4] Well, Obama turned out to be not a very good president, and I certainly am glad for David's reputation as a serious Washington sage that when they met, Senator Obama was not wearing panty hose.

No, not until now has anyone made the case for calling Obama a pallbearer, but from the preceding chapters it is clear: Obama is the pallbearer for American Liberalism.

Others rang up huge debts on the government's tab, but the great Republic could always manage. Not now—the outstanding debt to the Baby Boomers is overwhelming, and all that the zombies led by Obama can do is appropriate a trillion here and a trillion there. Then in Obamacare and Dodd-Frank we see the outlines of what lies ahead if Obama were to endure: Friendly Fascism. The Founders' edifice is finished. "We have given you a Republic if you can keep it," Benjamin Franklin informed an inquiring lady in Philadelphia as the Constitution was being wrapped up.

I say, once again we will keep it. The election of 2010 shows that we can keep it. Americans from all walks of life are turning out to affirm the Constitution, to once again defend American freedom, to safeguard free markets. They are the conservatives, the moderates, the independents, and many who have never shown an interest in politics in their lives. They know that we are at a climatic juncture in our history. Something is alive in the land: the Constitution. And something is dead: Liberalism.

NOTES

Introduction

1. Sir William Harcourt quoted in Harold Cox, *Economic Liberty* (Charleston, SC: BiblioLife, 2009), 170.
2. William F. Buckley Jr., *Up from Liberalism* (New York: McDowell, Obolensky Inc., 1959), xiv.

Chapter One

1. Oleg Troyanovsky, "The Making of Soviet Foreign Policy," in William Taubman et al., eds., *Nikita Khrushchev: The Man and His Era* (New Haven, Connecticut: Yale University Press, 2000), 231.
2. David Reynolds, *America, Empire of Liberty* (New York: Basic Books, 2009), 366.
3. Jon Meacham, "We Are All Socialists Now," *Newsweek*, February 7, 2009.
4. See "A Chorus of Millions" on YouTube, http://www.youtube .com/watch?v=tsrgYvx7KJE&feature=player_embedded.
5. Eric Hoffer, *The Temper of Our Time* (New York: Harper & Row, 1967), 18.

Chapter Two

1. Michelle Greene, "Boys' Night Out in Palm Beach," *People*, April 22, 1991, http://www.people.com/people/archive /article/0,,20114953,00.html.
2. Ibid.
3. Though he ran in 1980 and contemplated a run in 1984.

4. "Jesse Jackson's 'Hymietown' Remark—1984," *Washington Post*, http://www.washingtonpost.com/wp-srv/politics /special/clinton/frenzy/jackson.htm.

5. Hector Tobar and Eric Slater, "Sadness, Cries of Hypocrisy Greet Jackson's Disclosure About Child," *Los Angeles Times*, January 19, 2001, articles.latimes.com/2001/jan/19/news /mn-14325.

6. R. Emmett Tyrrell, Jr., "Remembering Clinton and the Episodic Apologists," Townhall.com, February 24, 2011, http:// townhall.com/columnists/emmetttyrrell/2011/02/24 /remembering_clinton_and_the_episodic_apologists/page /full/.

7. John F. Harris, *The Survivor: Bill Clinton in the White House* (New York: Random House, 2005), 111.

8. "Between Two Eras," *New York Times*, editorial, February 11, 2001, A16.

9. R. Emmett Tyrrell, Jr., "Clinton and the episodic apologists: After a decade, president's defenders still rise to the occasion," *Washington Times*, February 23, 2011, http://www .washingtontimes.com/news/2011/feb/23/clinton-and-the -episodic-apologists/.

10. "Clinton Corruption Plays Us for Fools—We Won't Forget," *New York Observer*, February 28, 2001), http://www.observer .com/2001/03/clinton-corruption-plays-us-for-foolswe -wont-forget-2/.

11. MSNBC, February 21, 2011.

12. facultystaff.richmond.edu/~ebolt/history398 /johnkerrytestimony.html.

13. ranker.com/list/republican-sex-scandals/web-infoguy.

14. "Pelosi Says Republican Budget 'Out of Whack,'" House Democratic Leader Nancy Pelosi news release, May 17, 2006, http://www.emailthecongress.com/news/05-17-pelosi-says -republican-budget-out-of-whack. Site no longer active.

15. Mark Leibovich, "The Comparison That Ends the Conversation," *Washington Post*, June 22, 2005.

16. Associated Press, April 20, 2007. See "Reid: Iraq War Lost, U.S. Can't Win," http://www.msnbc.msn.com/id/18227928/ns /politics/t/reid-iraq-war-lost-us-cant-win/.

17. Woodrow Wilson, *The New Freedom: A Call for the Emancipation of the Generous Energies of a People*, available online at http://www.gutenberg.org/ebooks/14811.

18. Peter Berkowitz, "Obama and the State of Progressivism," *Policy Review* no. 164, December 1, 2010, http://www.hoover .org/publications/policy-review/article/57971.

19. Herbert Croly, *The Promise of American Life* (New York: Macmillan, 1909), 276 (emphasis added).

20. "Clinton plays up Obama's 'bitter' quote as 'elitist,'" *USA Today*, April 14, 2008, www.usatoday.com/news/politics /election2008/2008-04-13-obama-clinton_N.htm.

Chapter Three

1. Eleanor Roosevelt, *This Is My Story* (New York: Harper and Brothers, 1937), 151.

2. Bernard Asbell, *Mother & Daughter: The Letters of Eleanor and Anna Roosevelt* (New York: Coward, McCann & Geoghegan, 1982), 20.

3. Clark Clifford, Memo to Harry S. Truman, November 19, 1947.

4. Henry Wallace, "Jobs, Peace, Freedom," *New Republic*, December 16, 1946, 785–89.

5. William Harlan Hale, "What Makes Wallace Run?" *Harper's*, March 1948, 241–48.

6. James A. Hagerty, "Wallace Rejected by Clothing Union," *New York Times*, December 18, 1947, 35.

7. See http://www.sourcewatch.org/index.php?title=Politics_of _personal_destruction.

8. Alonzo Hamby, *Beyond the New Deal: Harry S. Truman and American Liberalism* (New York: Columbia University Press, 1973), 277.

9. Max Ascoli, "What We Stand For," *Reporter*, December 20, 1949, 2.

10. Arthur M. Schlesinger Jr., *The Vital Center* (Boston: Houghton Mifflin, 1949), 256.
11. Ibid., 156.
12. Ibid., 223–24.

Chapter Four

1. Toby Harndon, "Barack Obama: 'Arrogant US Has Been Dismissive' to Allies," *Daily Telegraph*, April 3, 2009, http://www.telegraph.co.uk/news/worldnews barackobama/5100338/Barack-Obama-arrogant-US-has-been-dismissive-to-allies.html.
2. Reynolds, *America, Empire of Liberty, 357.*
3. Alonzo L. Hamby, *Liberalism and Its Challengers* (New York: Oxford University Press, 1985), 277.
4. Theodore H. White, *The Making of the President—1972* (New York: Atheneum, 1973), 34 (emphasis added).
5. Ibid., 22–23.
6. Ibid., 116.
7. James Piereson, "Investing in Conservative Ideas," *Commentary*, May 2005, 49.
8. White, *Making of the President*, 46–47.
9. Sean Wilentz, *The Age of Reagan: A History, 1974–2008* (New York: Harper 2008), 92.

Chapter Five

1. Michael Kazin, "Whatever Happened to the American Left?" *New York Times* Sunday Review, September 25, 2011, 4.
2. Stéphane Courtois et al., *The Black Book of Communism: Crimes, Terror, Repression*, Mark Kramer, cons. ed.; Jonathan Murphy and Mark Kramer, transs. (Cambridge, MA: Harvard University Press, 1999), 4.
3. Lester G. Crocker, *Jean-Jacques Rousseau: The Quest, 1712–1758* (New York: Macmillan, 1968), 160.
4. Letter to Engles, July 30, 1862, in Karl Marx, *Karl Marx, Friedrich Engels Werke* (East Berlin, 1956–1968) vol. 30, 259.
5. Mark Coppenger, *Moral Apologetics for Contemporary Christians* (Nashville: BH Publishing Group, 2011), 94.

6. Paul Johnson, *Intellectuals* (New York: Harper & Row, 1988; Phoenix Press, 2000), 27. Citations refer to the Phoenix edition.
7. Ibid., 18.
8. Ibid.
9. Ibid.
10. Ibid., 4
11. Ibid.
12. Croly, *Promise of American Life, 276.*
13. "The Doctrine of Fascism," by Benito Mussolini, 1932, from Michael J. Oakeshott's *The Social and Political Doctrine of Contemporary Europe* (Cambridge, England: Cambridge University Press, 1939), 164–68.
14. Johnson, *Intellectuals*, 26.
15. Robert Payne, *Marx* (New York: Simon & Schuster, 1968), 251.
16. Ibid.
17. Jakob Herman Huizinga, *The Making of a Saint* (London: H. Hamilton, 1976), 50.
18. Johnson, *Intellectuals*, 56.
19. Ibid., 67.
20. Leslie R. Page, *Karl Marx and the Critical Examination of His Works* (London: Freedom Association, 1987), 46–49.

Chapter Six

1. http://www.washingtonpost.com/wp-srv/politics/special/clinton/frenzy/hart2.htm.
2. Hillary Clinton interviewed on Fox News by James Rosen, February 20, 2009.
3. Andrew Roberts, "Among the Hagiographers," *Wall Street Journal*, March 26, 2011, http://online.wsj.com/article/SB10001424052748703529004576160371482469358.html.
4. Cass Sunstein, "The Visionary Minimalist," *New Republic*, January 30, 2008, 76, http://www.tnr.com/article/the-visionary-minimalist.
5. Cass Sunstein, "The Empiricist Strikes Back," *New Republic*, September 10, 2008, 77, http://www.tnr.com/article/the-empiricist-strikes-back.

6. Berkowitz, "Obama and the State of Progressivism."
7. Croly, *Promise of American Life*, 276.
8. Berkowitz, "Obama and the State of Progressivism."

Chapter Seven

1. Newsbusters.org/blogs/brad-wilmouth/2008/05/15
   /olbermann-accuses-bush-murderous-deceit-should-shut-hell.
2. http://krugman.blogs.nytimes.com/2009/07/06
   /administrative-costs/?pagemode=print.
3. http://krugman.blogs.nytimes.com/2011/04/06/paul
   -ryans-multiple-unicorns/.
4. Lionel Trilling, *The Liberal Imagination* (New York: New York
   Review of Books, 1950), xv.
5. Steve Kornacki, "When toxicity is a political strategy," *Salon.
   com*, May 2011, http://www.salon.com/2011/05/31
   /medicare-ryan.
6. This is a term lifted from the title of my 1992 book, *The
   Conservative Crack-Up*, which was widely misunderstood.
   I did diagnose the conservatives' condition as enfeebled
   by petty rivalries, but they would endure. As for Liberals,
   when I wrote *The Liberal Crack-Up* I was more pessimistic,
   and almost three decades later my pessimism has been
   vindicated.
7. Lois Romano, "GOP cashes in on poll success in states,"
   Washington Post, April 24, 2011, A3.
8. Exit poll data, CNN.com, November 3, 2010. See http://www
   .cnn.com/ELECTION/2010/results/polls.main/.
9. Exit poll data, CNN.com, November 5, 2008.
10. Henry Olsen, "Day of the Democratic Dead," *National Review
    Online*, November 1, 2010, www.nationalreview.com
    /articles/251670/day-democratic-dead-henry-olsen.
11. White, *Making of the President—1972*, 41.
12. Fox News brings in more revenue than the combined
    revenues of CNN, MSNBC, and the news broadcasts of the
    networks, ABC, CBS, and NBC.

ABOUT THE AUTHOR

R. Emmett Tyrrell, Jr., is founder and editor-in-chief of the famous and feared *American Spectator*, a political and cultural monthly, which has been published since 1967. He is the author of twelve books, including the *New York Times* best-selling *Boy Clinton: The Political Biography*. His other books include: *Public Nuisances*; *The Future That Doesn't Work: Social Democracy's Failures in Britain*, ed.; *Report on Network News' Treatment of the 1972 Democratic Candidates*, ed.; *The Liberal Crack-Up*; *Orthodoxy: The American Spectator's 20th Anniversary Anthology*, ed.; *The Conservative Crack-Up*; *The Impeachment of William Jefferson Clinton* (with Anonymous); *Madam Hillary: The Dark Road to the White House* (with Mark W. Davis); *The Clinton Crack-Up: The Boy President's Life After The White House*; *After the Hangover: The Conservatives' Road to Recovery*; and *The Best of The American Spectator's Continuing Crisis*. Tyrrell's nationally syndicated column is published weekly in such papers as the *New York Post*,

Los Angeles Times, Arizona Republic, Washington Times, and the *Washington Examiner.* Additionally, his writings have appeared in the *Wall Street Journal, Harper's,* the *New York Times, National Review, New York Magazine,* and the *Spectator* of London.

INDEX

democracy, 56
Democratic Party, 58
    affirmative action and, 71
    change, 105
    leadership decline, 72–73
    losses in 2010, 161
    New Politics Liberalism in, 77–78
    in 1970s, 8–9
    tears of, 54
democrats, Progressives as, 35
denial, 36
Dewey, John, 34
d'Houdetot, Sophie Countess, 90
dialogue
    expectation of, 123
    lack of, 129,130
    Liberal idea of, 125
Diderot, Denis, 88
disagreement, 38
    response to, 36
Discours sur l'inégalité (Rousseau), 92
Disraeli, Benjamin, 11
distinction, vs. notoriety, 107
disturbing the peace, 113
Dodd, Christopher, 23, 155
Dodd-Frank Act, 148, 154–58
    example of controls, 159–61
Dohrn, Bernardine, 87, 104
Drinan, Robert F., 77
Durbin, Richard, 32

E
earned-income credit, 152
economic reconstruction, 56
Edwards, John, 29, 107
Eisenhower, Dwight, 6, 64
election of 1946, 44
election of 1972, results, 76–77
election of 2010, 110, 136, 161
Emanuel, Rahm, 147
empathy, 116–17
Engels, Friedrich, 88

Enlightenment, 117
entitlement crisis, 16
entitlements, 150–52
entrepreneurism, 64
Environmental Defense Fund, 76
environmentalists, xiv
euthanasia, 113
evangelicals, 144

F
fairness, 117
Fannie Mae, 155, 158
Farbstein, Leonard, 77
fascism, 45, 47, 161
    Schlesinger on, 55–56
    vs. socialism, 149
federal government, approval rating in
    2011, 136–37
Federalist Number 10, 34
Financial Crisis Inquiry Commission
    (FCIC), 156
financial system
    federal regulation and, 156–57
    reform, 142
food stamps, 146, 151
force, in foreign policy, 56–57
Ford, Gerald R., 66
foreign policy
    of FDR, 63–64
    Schlesinger on, 56
40 More Years: How Democrats
    Will Rule the Next Generation
    (Carville), 132n
Founding Fathers, ix, xi, 11, 33, 99
    and human nature, 34
    for Liberalism, 83–84
    Progressives and, 33, 34
Four Freedoms, 64
Fox News, 139
Frank, Barney, 21, 155
Franklin, Benjamin, ix, 168
Freddie Mac, 155, 158

INDEX

INDEX

"Red Scare," 48
Reform Commission, 69
regulations, 148
Reich, Robert, 26
religious right, 144
Republican Party
    political candidates, 107
    Wilderness Years, 15
Reuther, Walter, 7, 48, 51
Reynolds, David, *America, Empire of Liberty*, 65
Richardson, Bill, 107
Roosevelt, Eleanor, 41–42, 57, 146
Roosevelt, Franklin D., 10, 50, 57, 63–64, 98
    and campaigning, 103
    death, 44
    Four Freedoms, 5
Roosevelt, Theodore, 34, 103
Rorty, Richard, 115, 116, 117-18
Rose, Alex, 48, 51
Ross, Irwin, 53
    Strategy for Liberals, 52, 146
Rousseau, Jean-Jacques, 11, 83–84, 85–86, 89–94, 97, 98
    Confessions, 91
    Discours sur l'inégalité, 92
    Emile, 90–92
    ideal state, 93
    Narcisse, 92
    personality, 90
    work and lifestyle, 87–88
Rovere, Richard, 6
Ryan, Paul, 124–25

S

"Sage *manqué*," 84–85
Sanford, Mark, 30
Sanford, Terry, 107
scandal, escape from consequences, 24–26
"scarcity economics," 47

Schechter poultry case, 63
Schlesinger, Arthur M., 51, 55–57, 67, 72
    The Vital Center, 7, 52
Secret Knowledge: On the Dismantling of American Culture, The (Marmet), 11
secular intellectual, 84–85
separation of powers, 34
Sharpton, Al, 25
Sinclair, Upton, 33
Smith, Gerald L. K., 50
Snow, Edgar, 165
social engineering, Rousseau and, 93
social reforms, of FDR, 64
Social Security, 151–52
socialism, xi
    vs. fascism, 149
South of 1940s, 57–58
Spitzer, Eliot, 28
"spreading prosperity," xi
Stalin, Joseph, 45
stealth socialists, 12, 115, 139, 148
Stowe, Leland, 53
    Target: You, 52
Straight, Michael, 43
Strategy for Liberals (Ross), 52, 146
Streisand, Barbra, 36
students, 4
Sunstein, Cass, 115–16
Supplemental Security Income, 152
Supreme Court, FDR and, 63
Swift Boat Veterans for Truth, 29

T

Tanenhaus, Sam, *The Death of Conservatism*, 16, 131–33
Taranto, James, 124
Target: You (Stowe), 52
taxes, 31, 137, 150
    Infantile Leftists and, 113
Tea Party movement, 15, 137

INDEX